A Long Way Home

The Story of a
Jewish Youth, 1939–1949

Bob Golan

Edited by Jacob Howland
With a Preface by Bette Howland

To Larry & Joy
with best
Bob

18/05

D0913733

UNIVERSITY PRESS OF AMERICA,® INC.
Lanham • Boulder • New York • Toronto • Oxford

Copyright © 2005 by
University Press of America,® Inc.
4501 Forbes Boulevard
Suite 200
Lanham, Maryland 20706
UPA Acquisitions Department (301) 459-3366

PO Box 317
Oxford
OX2 9RU, UK

Library of Congress Control Number: 2004115706
ISBN 0-7618-3039-1 (paperback : alk. ppr.)

This book is dedicated to my wife Shirley, my sons
Michael and Gary, my daughter-in-law Ilana,
and my grandchildren Rachel and David.

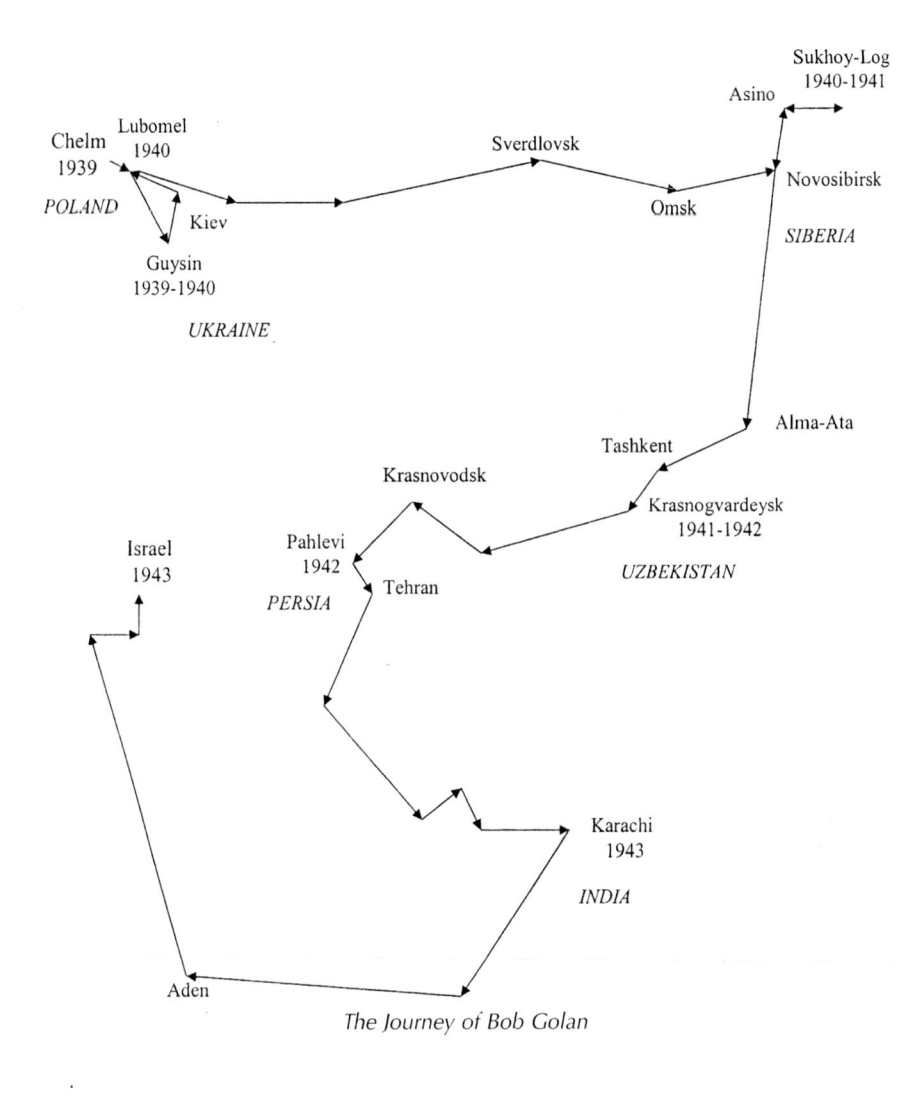

The Journey of Bob Golan

Contents

Preface

The City of Chelm, where this story begins, lies just west of the Bug River, a natural border separating Poland from what was the Soviet Union. Not all borders are natural; over its long history Chelm belonged to Austria, to Russia, and was occupied twice in two World Wars by Germany. And, once upon a time, it was the most renowned of all towns in Yiddish folklore—home to the fabled Wise Men of Chelm.

As the Angel of the Lord (so the story goes) flew over the earth, sowing seeds equally of wisdom and folly, a mishap occurred; the bag full of folly got dumped over Chelm. That was its claim to fame. "Wise Men" became a term of derision, and "Chelmer" synonymous with simpleton. If daily life was a riddle—to be solved at great length, with the most tortuous logic and hapless results—just think of Chelmers lost in the world. In a typical tale, they venture forth collecting alms for a new bath-house, necessary in Jewish ritual, and their efforts meet with success. But what to do with the money? The forests are deep, pitch-black at night, prowling with wolves, robbers, and worse; their lives and their pockets aren't safe. So they exchange the gold for feathers, which, scattered to the winds, will be borne gently back to Chelm. Everyone needs feathers. With empty barrels, bushel baskets, aprons spread wide and eyes raised on high, Chelmers await their windfall.

Jews are no strangers to journeys. Throughout the millennia they have been major disseminators of folklore from all over the place; but the stories of Chelm probably sprang from sources close by—the Holy Fool of East European legend, unfortunates protected only by God. Jews turned this romantic and superstitious idea into a joke, characteristically, a joke on themselves —poking fun at bearded elders, commentaries upon commentaries, deliberations without end, nit-picking reasoning of Talmud and Pilpul. These tales hide a bitter truth. The Jews of Chelm were *Ostjuden*. Ever trying to determine what God wanted from them, ever waiting with eyes raised on high, theirs was a way of life extreme both in poverty and piety. Even to their fellow Jews they belonged to a world apart. They knew the languages of their surroundings and the Hebrew of Torah, but the words of their own intimate speech were Yiddish, the Mother Tongue. The Chelm of story was a never-never land, out of time, out of place—only another name for exile. Exile had many names, and those names and places and people are now known as a vanished world.

In Bob Golan's memoir the Chelm of 1939 could be the Chelm of 1900. His father is a cobbler, the family—there's a younger brother—lives in one room, both shop and home, on the ground floor of a large apartment building. Water comes from a pump, light from kerosene lamps; chickens, geese, and ducks run loose in the courtyard, children play barefoot to save their shoes, and of the four outhouses, two—provided with locks and squares of newspaper—are reserved for wealthier tenants, who live on floors higher up. Resourceful, inventive, Israel Goldman (as he was then) fashions toys out of scraps from trash heaps; darts and a blowgun; a flashlight/lantern; a pair of skates. He's not particularly aware that his family is poor: most are, Poles as well as Jews. Though it must be said that after school and on sacred holy days the Jews do not gang up to throw rocks at the Poles.

On September 1, 1939, not two weeks after his 12th birthday, excitement comes to sleepy Chelm. The Germans and the Russians have signed a pact to carve up Poland between them. From the West, German bombs; from the East, Russian tanks; ones that mean business. The Polish army, with its horse-drawn artillery and tiny toy tanks, is defeated in no time. Suddenly everyone is from Chelm.

There must have been a glitch in the pact: the Russian invaders pull back, East, beyond the Bug; anyone who wants can go with them. Go? Stay? Caught in between, his family tries to get home, but it's too late; they have to go. A decisive piece of luck. Of the four camps built strictly for killing, three—Belzec, Sobibor and Treblinka—would occupy that short stretch of border along the Bug.

For the Germans arbitrariness was a deliberate and calculated policy, a weapon; for the Russians it was a shrug. They had no Solution; they just didn't know what to do with all the desperate souls now on their hands, so the first thing they did was arrest them. On his next birthday, his 13th, Golan's mother will take him to a man, maybe a Rabbi, maybe not, who will teach him a few blessings and mutter a few prayers. Only later will the boy realize that this forbidden ceremony, in a Siberian labor camp, has been his Bar Mitzvah.

Golan's memoir is taken from notes made at the time, in Russian, and first written up not long after, in Hebrew. Don't let anyone tell you that Holocaust memoirs are all alike; each is a pair of eyes. Children are a special kind of witness. They have a keen sense of cruelty and injustice, but, since these things usually exist in inverse ratio, little or no power and control over their lives. Simon Srebnik, at thirteen one of two survivors of the killing camp at Chelmno, and before that the years of the Lodz ghetto, had seen little of life but death. I didn't understand, he says, I thought it was normal. What's normal? Children are all eyes: how can they question what they see?

This is a perilous journey with no destination. Sealed boxcars; Russian trucks fuelled by wood-stove—this is not a land of plenty; horse-carts; barges so overloaded with bundles and bodies if they don't sit still they'll sink. Everywhere it's the same story; armies of refugees, vermin, disease; never enough food or shelter; and among these masses of displaced persons, no one knows where they're going. Golan's strong and self-reliant parents are beside themselves with worry, fearful for their children, burdened with making choices when they can only take chances. Always hungry, always dirty— always something—Golan, the big brother, is still resourceful; fashioning skis and fishing poles, cooking up schemes to outwit the soup kitchen ration system. A 1 on a coupon can become a 4; and if a 4, why not a 7? Why not a 10? He's only a boy, and he's seeing the world. First this happens, then that, and then the next thing. The way it is is the way it must be.

In the end, his story is a *Bildungsroman*. There is a destination after all, and by the time they reach it, parents and children will find themselves, inevitably, worlds apart. Some things though never change. In a refugee camp after the War, the Poles, who have suffered so terribly its devastations, are still throwing rocks at the Jews.

Almost all of Chelm's 15,000 Jews were murdered in the camps along the Bug. Sobibor and Treblinka, partially destroyed in prisoner revolts, were blown up, dug up, ploughed and planted with trees. Memory, too, must be exterminated. On the grassy site that was Treblinka thousands upon thousands of rocks hewn from a nearby quarry bear witness to the villages, cities and towns all over Poland whose dead have no memorials. And Chelm? With a population around six figures, it's the capital of the province, the thriving center of this fertile agricultural region. Does anyone recall its former fame? The once-upon-a-time people have vanished; there are surely no Wise Men in Chelm. And anyway there are worse things than being a fool. As Golan learns in the course of his journey, "it's better to be lucky than smart."

Bette Howland

Acknowledgements

The author and editor would like to acknowledge the kind assistance of several people. Shirley Golan brought a keen critical eye to the text and saved us from many errors. We are grateful for her tireless support and encouragement. Without Moshe Goldman, this story would not be what it is. John and Betty Redding provided helpful advice. Brad Bradley of the Department of History at the University of Tulsa checked the spelling and translation of Russian phrases, and Bette Howland proofread the text and offered sound literary advice. Finally, we would like to thank the Chapman Trusts for a generous publication subvention, and Dean Tom Benediktson of the University of Tulsa College of Arts and Sciences for permission to use Chapman funds for this purpose.

Chapter One

Child of Chelm

I was born on August 20, 1927, to Shayndl and Wolf Goldman of Chelm, Poland. My name was Israel Goldman, but everybody called me by my Polish nickname, Srulik. I called my parents Mama and Tata (or when I was older, Papa), and Moshe, my younger brother, I called Moishele.

Except for the singular distinction of fame, the people of my hometown were no different from those residing in other small communities in Eastern Poland. This fame was not welcomed by the Jewish residents of Chelm, but nonetheless it spread across Eastern Europe by way of Jewish literature, humor, and folklore, including in particular the well-known stories of Sholom Aleichem. The tales told about us depicted a community baffled by its surroundings. The dilemmas that arose in these tales, and the solutions arrived at by the assembly of Jewish leaders, were both comic and unrealistic. The community leaders—derisively known as *Chelmeh Khokhomim*, "Wise Men of Chelm"—were invariably shown to be out of their depth, as was the entire Jewish community. A resident of Chelm, known as a "Chelmer," became a byword for a simpleton.

I don't think our reputation was justified. But in any case, I know now that it is more important to be lucky than smart.

Chelm lies near the Bug River, which is now the eastern border that separates Poland from Belarus and Ukraine. It is in the region that the Soviets occupied right after the outbreak of the Second World War. In 1939, which is more or less when my story begins, Poland extended far east of the Bug. But at the start of the war, the Soviet army drove all the way to Warsaw and the Wistula River. Things would have turned out worse for us if we'd lived in the west, which was seized by the Germans immediately after they invaded our country.

1

In 1939, there were about 15,000 of us Jews in Chelm. This number represented half of the total population of the city. The Jewish community of Chelm
had several synagogues and schools, an old age home, and an orphanage. There
were even two Jewish weeklies. The rest of the population consisted of Roman
Catholics and a small number of Greek Orthodox. Some of the Jews lived in an
exclusively Jewish section of the town, which by present American standards
would be considered a slum. The majority of the population, however, lived in
neighborhoods of mixed religions. Ours was such a mixed neighborhood.

Except for the fact that it unfolded in a vanished world, my childhood was
rather ordinary. Our building had three stories. The ground floor, where we
lived, housed the poorest tenants. The upper floors usually housed clerks,
bookkeepers, government officials, teachers and low-ranking army officers
and their families. Our home was a long one-room apartment facing a cobblestone street. In the center of our building there was a large courtyard with
a row of storage sheds in which the tenants kept wood or coal for cooking and
heating. Some of the tenants also raised chickens, ducks, and geese that
roamed the courtyard during the day and were kept in the sheds at night.

The cobblestone courtyard was also a playground for us children. We
learned to hop around the droppings from the birds and to watch out for the
geese, which were always nipping at our legs. The situation was more an-
noying during the summer months, when most of us ran around barefoot in
order to save our shoes for the winter.

We played soccer and volleyball in the courtyard, and also something called
twin camp ball. Twin camp ball involved two opposing lines of players throwing a ball at each other with a team captain in front. The team captain would hurl
the ball at the opposing team, and if a player did not catch it, he was out. The
game continued until a team ran out of players. We could not afford a real ball,
so we improvised by making a core from old newspapers wrapped with rags,
which were then tied with string to keep the ball from falling apart.

My favorite pastime was playing army. We made bows and arrows from the
nearby chestnut trees, and I made a blow-dart gun from some old conduit pipe
by fastening the pipe on a stock cut out from a board. I fashioned the darts
from drill bits retrieved from the trash can of a dentist who lived two doors
down the street. From my father's shoe-repair trash, I retrieved soft leather
strips to wrap around the dentist's drill bits. I ground the drill bit point on the
pavement to sharpen it, and for the "poison" I dipped the point in iodine
mixed with kerosene, just the way the natives did it in the movies and the adventure books that I loved to read.

My father was a cobbler who repaired shoes and made boots for Polish officers. His shop was located in our apartment. On one side of the apartment
was our dining room table, a wooden bench, and two chairs, as well as one

twin bed and a closet where we kept our Sabbath clothes. At bedtime my mother used to take the straw mattress that was stored on my parents' bed during the day, and put it on top of the dining table for Moshe and me to sleep on. We loved to sleep on this improvised bed because it was so high up, and we used to pretend to be pilots in an airplane.

On the other side of the apartment there was a brick stove made for burning coal or wood for cooking and heating. We never had running water or electricity. The landlord had contracted for electricity to be wired, but the war broke out before they got around to doing it. In the meantime we used a kerosene lamp for light at night, and our drinking water came from a hand pump about a hundred yards down the street. It was my responsibility to see to it that the eight-gallon, porcelain-coated bucket was always full. My reward for delivering the water was a promise by my mother that I would develop big muscles in my arms. I was a skinny boy, and to me having big muscles sounded like a pretty good idea.

As for our toilet, we had four outhouses that stood near the sheds in the courtyard and next to the communal garbage box. Two of the outhouses were exclusively for use by our richer neighbors, and these were always locked. The other two outhouses were open for the rest of us tenants. I preferred to use the locked ones because they were cleaner, and for toilet paper they had newspapers cut up into squares.

To get inside the locked toilets I used to climb over the top of the door. On occasion I would get caught and receive a scolding, but that never stopped me. Our building janitor, who was not a Jew, was drunk most of the time but kept the area fairly clean. His son Manyek was one of my playmates. Manyek was the only non-Jewish kid in our building who spoke fluent Yiddish, the language of most of the Jews of Eastern Europe.

Moshe and I had two living grandmothers as well as many aunts, uncles, and cousins. Our grandfathers died before I was born. These relatives would often visit (and vice-versa), and then we would be treated to cakes and cookies.

On Fridays my mother would give us our weekly scrubbing in a big tub made of galvanized metal. Then she would sprinkle us with some of her perfume, and dress us in our best and only finery for the traditional Sabbath dinner. On Saturday, my father would take me and Moshe to the nearby synagogue for Sabbath services. There we would meet my uncle Wolf Feldman, my father's brother-in-law and also his best friend. My maternal grandmother Naomi often came over to help my mother prepare lunch for the men when they returned from the synagogue. After the meal we would sometimes go out to the countryside with Wolf and his wife Frieda for a picnic or a swim in the Uherka creek. At other times my father invited his buddies over to play dominoes, while my mother served refreshments and visited with their wives.

I loved the various seasons of the year. During the fall and winter when the nights were long, I made a lantern to light my way at night by cutting off the bottom of a transparent bottle and attaching to it a lid from a jar secured with rope around the neck of the bottle. I used a nail, with a rock for a hammer, to punch holes in the jar lid. Then I placed a lit candle inside the bottle, which became a functional "flashlight." I also made my own ice skates by strapping a quarter-inch steel rod to a block of wood and securing the skates to my shoes with rope. I had fun on those skates just knowing that they were made by me. I usually skated on the street, but sometimes I would sneak inside the school across the street and use the man-made rink. I liked to ski, too, but I had no skis of my own. At the end of the day, during the long winter evenings, my father would tell us stories of his childhood. Sometimes he would read to us from *Sabina*, a weekly romance novel to which he subscribed.

From the time I was in the first grade, I attended a state-run primary school named Koszciuszko. Koszciuszko was a public school, not a parochial one, but it was nonetheless a thoroughly Catholic institution. It was one of three schools located in a new building on the outskirts of town. Koszciuszko was on the first floor, and on the second floor was a Jewish primary school named Clara. My parents didn't send me to this Jewish school because they thought the public school would provide a better education.

In many ways, I liked Koszciuszko. The school playground was a good size. We used it mostly for games and exercise in the summer. In the winter, we used the steep hill across from the school for skiing and sledding. The classrooms were large, accommodating fifty-two students comfortably (two per bench), and plenty of light came through the big windows. Discipline was strict: we spoke only when given permission, and during lectures we sat with our hands behind our backs.

My homeroom teacher was an attractive young lady who happened to live in our building and was a customer of my father. We also had a very strict arithmetic teacher who was Jewish. One time, as a punishment for not memorizing the multiplication table to his satisfaction, he made me stand for a whole hour facing the classroom wall. After that I memorized the table to the point where I could recite it in my sleep. The only other Jewish teacher I had taught Bible study. He was assigned to all of the Jewish kids in the school — about seven of us. This was a relaxed class with free discussion. The rest of my teachers were Roman Catholics.

Anti-Semitism was rampant in my school. Every morning before class, all the students had to line up facing a large cross with Jesus on it and recite a prayer. The Jewish students, officially registered as "Of the Faith of Moses," were not required to recite this prayer, but we did have to line up with everyone else. Often we were kicked or punched from behind by some boy demanding that we pray to Jesus. One time I turned around and kicked back, and got into a fight right in the middle of the prayer. The other boy and I were both taken to the principal's office, but only I was reprimanded. I had to bring my mother to the school so the principal could tell her that I had misbehaved. ·

Another favorite place for discrimination was the boy's restroom. There the difference between those who were circumcised and those who were not was obvious. The Catholic boys would sometimes urinate on a Jewish boy. They got away with it, unless the Jewish boy was big enough to pay them back in kind.

On several occasions the Catholic children and even some of their parents gathered after school to take turns kicking us and calling us Christ-killers. At such times I chose the long way home to avoid the gang, which entailed climbing an eight-foot fence to the high school grounds and going home through the rail yard. This added about three miles to my trip. I felt so helpless and angry about having to do this that I think I would have turned a gun on the gang if I'd had one.

Across the street from our apartment was a parochial school next to a Catholic church complex. Only rich Catholics attended that school. The students looked neat and well dressed, and most of them arrived at school in horse-drawn carriages or accompanied by servants. Occasionally, we Jewish kids vented our anger on those students by throwing frozen snow balls at them. Then their servants would chase us.

The parochial school was also surrounded by a six-foot wrought iron fence covered with wild berry vines. One time when we were playing army I shot an arrow into the vines on the fence. When I climbed the fence to retrieve the arrow, the school janitor came out with his street broom and struck me, causing me to fall and skin my knee. My father saw this happen. He ran over, punched the janitor in the nose, and told him to pick on someone his own size. Needless to say, the janitor filed suit. The hearing was held in the Municipal Court. We told the judge what had happened, and as evidence we showed him my bruised knee. The judge asked the janitor his religion. "Roman Catholic, of course," the janitor replied. Then the judge asked my father his religion, and he said "the faith of Moses, of course." The judge gave my father a stern look and fined him two Polish zloty (about a day's wages). My father was not very happy with this decision, and all the way home he was wishing bad things on the enemies of Israel. The janitor, on the other hand, became friendly to us. More than once, he invited us to his house and served us freshly pickled sauerkraut from a barrel. Maybe he felt guilty about hitting me with his broom.

Throughout my childhood, I received lessons from various rabbis about the Bible. Nothing was ever mentioned about Jesus or the Christian faith. Many years later I learned that the primary cause for anti-Semitism was the interpretation of the Christian Bible. In some parts of the Christian Bible, the crucifixion of Jesus is blamed on the Jews instead of the Romans. But it was the Romans who crucified Christ.

Once or twice I attended services in the Catholic church near us. It was interesting to watch the priests conduct the services and listen to the boys' choir singing amidst the tall candles and gold crosses. It was especially fascinating when the whole congregation formed a procession during Easter to march down the street. Little boys dressed in white aprons led the procession while tossing flower petals. Next came the priests and altar boys, holding church banners and crimson-colored pillows displaying the crown of thorns and other paraphernalia of the crucifixion. They also carried huge crosses alongside the pillows. The congregation followed, bearing lit candles and singing hymns.

I often asked my parents why the Catholics didn't like us. The reply was always the same: "What can you expect from a *Shaygits* (a mean non-Jew)?" It is probably a good thing that I did not know at the time that Jesus was also a Jew like me. That would really have made things hard to understand.

Most of the kids in my neighborhood were buddies with whom I played games and got into mischief, but my best friends were David Nankin and a fellow named Dzidek (whose last name I can no longer remember). David was a sweet boy and a top student in all subjects. He was also a true artist. He could draw landscapes and portraits of people to a perfect likeness, and he could do it in just a few minutes. I got my inspiration for drawing by watching him work. David's father had died a couple of years before I met him, but his mother did a splendid job bringing him up. His clothes were always clean, and so was their small apartment.

Dzidek, on the other hand, was a Greek Orthodox of Russian descent. His father was the general manager of the one and only lumber mill in the area, and their spacious house was on the premises of the mill. The mill, with its lumber yard and small trolleys, became the ideal place for our games of Cowboys and Indians. The neatly stacked boards were perfect for hide and seek.

Unfortunately for me, our play almost cost me an eye. Dzidek and I were attacking each other with long sticks that we had fashioned into spears. One of those spears accidentally struck me below my left eye. I ran home with my face covered with blood. When mother saw me she let out a scream that scared me more than the blood and the pain. She immediately washed my face, treated my wound with iodine (our "cure-all"), and bandaged my eye. The next day my eye became infected and all I could see was white. When I told my parents they became worried. My father immediately took me to a doctor whom he knew from his time in the army. The doctor put some medication into my eye, but that did not help very much. The eye swelled shut. In the meantime, the army doctor left town to join his unit for training exercises.

Mama took me to another eye doctor. This doctor seemed to be more concerned about the condition of my eye than the first one was, because he gave me a thorough examination and prescribed medication to be applied three times a day. He told me to come back in a week. After several treatments things improved. I began to distinguish objects, and gradually my vision returned to normal. Years later, another doctor told me that my left eye was weak. It needed corrective lenses long before the right one did.

About three blocks down our street was a slaughterhouse for hogs. Moshe and I used to watch the butcher make sausages. On various occasions we helped the butcher herd some of the hogs to the slaughter house. Some of them were huge and the butcher needed all the help he could get. As a reward, the butcher would give us kielbasa sausage. Moshe and I loved the taste and smell of the kielbasa. My father knew about the pig meat, and he let us hide the sausages under his workbench. Mama pretended not to know about it, but we had strict orders not to breathe even a word about it to Grandmother Naomi. Had my grandmother known, she never would have stepped into our house again.

My brother and I loved Naomi Shporer, as did everyone. I don't believe that she ever had any enemies. She was always willing to share with people less fortunate than herself. With a colorful scarf that covered her silver hair in the style of a babushka, she looked just like we thought a grandmother should. Her face, which was full of wrinkles etched by time and hardship, radiated love and goodness. She always greeted Moshe and me with a toothless smile and open arms. Naomi had been married twice but was widowed for the second time long before I was born, and she raised four daughters and one son by selling fruit. She would pick out the best fruit and hand it to Moshe and me, saying "for my grandchildren it has to be the best," and she would smile while we ate it.

The Germans, however, did not think as well of my grandmother as we did. A soldier shot her when she refused the order of the Nazi SS to vacate her house. She was sixty-seven years old, but she still managed to spit in the soldier's face before she died.

We loved my other grandmother, Gitl Goldman, too, but we were not as attached to her because she was away most of the time working as a pastry chef in a resort. Her husband Yisrael, after whom I am named, died in an accident at a vodka distillery when my father was twelve. A pressurized tank exploded, dousing him with hot liquid. His body blistered, and he ran to the nearby river to cool off. He died after the burns became infected. My father told me that he was a tall, strong man and a good father and husband. After his death, Grandma Gitl had to raise two girls and one boy by herself.

My father's sister Hendl lived with Gitl until she married Yitzhak Karp. When the Germans came, Yitzhak managed to elude one of the SS killing actions and cross the border into Russia. But my aunt Hendl, her twelve-month-old baby, and Grandma Gitl could not escape the German roundup. They were sent to the Sobibor death camp, where they were murdered by the SS.

In the summer of 1939, we walked out to the orchards, as we always did, to buy apples, pears, and gooseberries from the farmers. The hot dust felt good under my bare feet on the unpaved road. I was almost twelve years old—a boy on the verge of youth. This was to be my last summer in Chelm, and the beginning of a series of strange and fateful events that were to shape my life in unexpected and unimaginable ways.

Chapter Two

War and Flight

In May of 1939, I was promoted to the sixth grade of the Tadeusz Kosciuszko School. I was beginning to feel like an old hand. My parents had saved up some money, and Mama was making plans for me to go to high school and afterwards to study to become a dentist. We were also talking about traveling to Warsaw to visit Aunt Luba and her family, as we had done two years earlier. I was looking forward to the summer.

But all of our plans had an air of uncertainty. Our conversations invariably turned to politics. There was talk about a mobilization and alliances between England, Poland, and France. The year before, Poland had insisted that the Czechs surrender some disputed territory. The past March, however, Germany had made Czechoslovakia a vassal state.

All of this talk confused me. These things seemed to be happening so far away. I wondered why we couldn't go to visit Aunt Luba.

But there were also mysterious events closer to home.

There was a town idiot whom we kids used to tease. He walked around in tattered clothing and a sackcloth hood, and he carried a long thick pole. One day he was arrested and charged with espionage on behalf of the Germans. The police claimed that they had caught him in the act of photographing the location of the ammunition dump on the outskirts of town. The long pole, the police claimed, was hollow and contained maps and plans of military installations.

War was in the air. The Polish Air Force showed off their World War I biplanes in frequent flyovers. The civil defense had various drill exercises with gas masks and controlled explosions. One day, I was asked by an officer to participate in a simulated attack. My part was to pretend to be wounded. After a gas grenade was thrown, I ran into the smog and lay down on the ground.

Medics then rushed in with a stretcher and carried me out while photographers were taking pictures. There was much troop movement, and horse-drawn artillery rumbled through the streets.

It was all exciting to me, and it couldn't have come at a better time than my summer vacation. Martial music blared from the radios and the whole town had a festive air. To me, the Polish Army looked like it could beat any army in the world. My father was in the artillery reserves, so he explained to me how the horses were specially trained to pull the cannons and to avoid taking fright from explosions. He also showed me how the cannons were primed to fire.

The year before, the Poles had fallen into a trap by accepting part of Silesia, a northern Czech province, when it was offered to them by the Germans. Knowing full well that the Poles would never agree, the Germans subsequently demanded a passage through Poland from Germany to Prussia, a chunk of German territory lying north of Warsaw on the Baltic Sea. The whole chess game unraveled in August of 1939 when Germany and the Soviet Union signed a nonaggression pact. Germany was now free to attack Poland.

On September 1, 1939, less than two weeks after I turned twelve, the German army crossed the Polish border in a new style of warfare called *Blitzkrieg* that utilized lightning thrusts of mechanized as well as infantry divisions. They justified their invasion by means of a trumped-up charge about an attack on German border guards.

The day after the invasion began our local army barracks were attacked by German bombers. My buddies and I were up in the attic of our building watching the bombers dive and drop their ordinance on the barracks, which was about two miles away. The only anti-aircraft fire I saw was provided by Mr. Kucinski, our friendly district policeman, who shot his pistol into the air as the planes flew overhead. The exploding bombs sounded like a giant hammer banging on steel plates. A large section of the local army base was on fire, and thick black smoke was billowing into the sky. It all happened so fast that it did not seem real.

From that day on the war became part of our daily lives. The parochial school across the street was converted into a hospital, and columns of weary and wounded soldiers began to arrive at its doors. Our anti-aircraft units set up a couple of cannons in the school yard, and when the German planes flew over the cannons fired away, causing our windows to rattle. Throughout the entire war I did not see a single Polish aircraft engage the German bombers. We heard later on that the German Luftwaffe destroyed most of the Polish Air Force on the first day of the war, before our planes even had a chance to take off.

Food became scarce. The farmers were reluctant to bring produce to town because the German planes were strafing the roads. Bread and staple food-stuffs were rationed and shoppers had to wait in long lines. Food hoarding contributed to the shortages. The official Polish radio kept us informed about the battles on the various fronts. From the radio came such announcements as: "A large German unit was wiped out by the brave Polish Cavalry near the city." "The united front of Poland, France, and England will defeat the German swine on their own soil," the radio continued. "It is a matter of time until the war will be over with the defeat of the German aggressors . . ."

The Polish government began to mobilize reserve troops in three categories —A, B, and C. They called up categories A and B. My father, who was thirty-two at the time, was placed in category C. But Poland was defeated so quickly that he was never called up.

The German bombers intensified their raids and civilian buildings were not spared. One bomb hit a building about two blocks from our house. People said that it was aimed at the police station across the street, but the planes missed the target. Another bomb struck a few houses down from my Aunt Rachel's house. Moshe and I went over to check on her family and found a big, sharp piece of shrapnel embedded in a tree.

The hospital across the street began to overflow with patients, and many were laid up in the aisles or on the floor. The walking wounded had to wait their turn, as only emergency cases had priority for treatment. My family took in a soldier with a bullet lodged in his right elbow. It was several days before they could take care of him at the hospital. There was a shortage of food in the hospital, so we also shared some of our meals with the wounded. Some of the soldiers from the cavalry who had been sent to the hospital told us that they were ordered to attack advancing German tanks and were mowed down by machine gun fire.

I have no idea why the Germans spent so much time bombing Chelm, a seemingly non-strategic city. It became dangerous to remain in town. At the sound of the sirens announcing an air raid, we would grab our ready-made pack and leave for the outskirts of town to hide in the forest. My parents, together with my father's sister Frieda and her husband Wolf, ultimately decided to escape the bombings by moving out of the city to a nearby farm. We agreed to rent one room as well as the barn.

The farmer picked us up in town, loading us and our belongings onto a hay wagon drawn by two horses. The farmer's wife, a middle aged, plump woman, received us with a broad smile at their two-room cottage. Their farm-house had a thatched roof. The roof was supported by logs resting on thick walls made of mud reinforced with straw. The walls of the cottage were whitewashed inside and out. There was no electricity or running water.

The farmer's wife had cleared her daughter's room for us prior to our arrival. My aunt and uncle and my parents settled down on the compacted dirt floor to wait out the war. Moshe and I were given the barn, where we were to sleep on some straw. The farmer's daughter, a teenager, was moved into the attic and slept on straw as well.

The farm was about seven miles from town. Every day we watched the German bombers fly over us towards Chelm. As they dropped their bombs we could hear the explosions and see black smoke rise into the sky. There were rumors that one of the bombers was shot down and the crew captured as they floated down in their parachutes. With my own eyes, however, I saw only that the narrow cobblestone and dirt road was clogged with retreating Polish forces in utter disarray. In the west, the mechanized German advance tore the valiant Polish Army to shreds. The Poles suffered the same fate in the east from the advancing Soviet forces.

Soon the bombing stopped. We saw several planes fly over that were marked with the red star of the Soviet Union. They seemed to be reconnaissance flights. It looked like the war would soon be over and Poland would be vanquished.

Papa and Wolf walked to town to find out if it was safe to return. They came back and said that we could go back home. We loaded up the farmer's wagon, and he took us back to Chelm.

On the way into Chelm, some soldiers checked our identification papers. I felt elation and relief as we approached the outskirts of town. Our neighbors greeted us warmly, but everyone was worried about what was going to happen. There was a unit of soldiers sitting on the sidewalk with their back against our building. They seemed dead tired and hungry. One young soldier drew my attention because he seemed not much older than I was. I gave him a thick slice of bread and a cup of water. The soldier told me that he was from Warsaw. He was running from the Germans. His eyes were sad, and he looked frail as he clutched his machine gun. He thanked me for the bread and water and moved on.

The radio fell silent, with the exception of some messages in code. Poland was being squeezed from both sides at once. Occasionally an army unit stopped by for a brief rest and confirmed the rumors that Soviet tanks were moving in from the east.

Poland was capitulating. It was in the air. Everyone knew it, but no one believed it could have happened so fast. My parents and our neighbors were very worried about what was going to happen next. The uncertainty was exasperating.

Our neighbor, the wife of a sergeant who lived on the third floor of our building, told us that her husband had been captured by the Germans and was being held as a prisoner of war. But she seemed to be more worried about the Soviets than the Germans. Before the war her two lovely daughters had never so much as spoken to us, but now they were willing to play with us Jewish kids.

During the next few days our little town became flooded with Polish nobles and officials on their way south. They were making for the Romanian border. I collected quite a few tips directing their cars to the only filling station in town, one with a hand-operated pump. I waited for the cars on the outskirts of the city and asked the occupants if they needed gasoline. If they did, I jumped on the running board and directed them to the station.

The southbound traffic continued until the station ran out of gas. With no fuel to be found anywhere in Chelm, the automobile owners bought any horses they could get their hands on, hitched them to their cars, and had the horses tow them as far south as they could go.

For a day or two everything seemed quiet. There were no soldiers or traffic, and it seemed as if there was no longer any war. Only a couple of Soviet twin-engine planes flew over town. My father said that those were heavy bombers. I asked him how he knew and he said "they *sound* heavy." To me that was as good an answer as any.

The next morning we heard a loud rumble. I ran outside and saw five tanks with red stars on their gun turrets roaring down the street. They looked like huge monsters compared to the Polish tanks, which were only about my height. One of the tanks lost control while turning at the corner and slid into a building, tearing a chunk out of it.

The following day, the Polish communists erected a welcome gate for the Soviets, and lined the route along Lubelska Street with slogans and red banners. When everything was ready the main tank column began to roll in. The tanks kept coming and coming, two abreast, taking up the whole street. There seemed to be no end to it. Their tracks tore up the cobblestones, and the smoke from their engines filled the air. The tank commanders stood in their turrets wearing their padded helmets.

I had a good feeling about these Soviets. They seemed to exude strength and security. I was puzzled about the fears of our neighbor, the sergeant's wife. They seemed friendly enough to me.

The tanks were followed by infantrymen. The soldiers were sitting on benches in big trucks holding rifles with long, narrow bayonets. Those bayonets scared me.

Finally, in came the artillery, drawn by trucks. What a contrast to the Polish horse-drawn artillery! I felt disappointed in my father's army. No wonder Poland had lost the war in just three weeks.

The arrival of the Soviets enabled the local communists to take over the city administration. The new government's first order of business was the release of all political prisoners and the establishment of a police force to keep law and order. The new police force, whose officers could be identified by their red armbands, was made up of former communist prisoners. The authorities also promptly incarcerated all of the former jailers and policemen.

To a twelve year old boy, all of this was exciting. I ran from place to place to see what was happening. I stood next to the tanks, felt their steel, examined the cannons, and listened to our new masters speaking Russian. Soviet soldiers filled the city and they were buying everything in sight, especially wrist watches. In many cases they paid with IOUs, which were worthless because they could not be redeemed. The Soviet propaganda machine shifted into gear, and commissars were everywhere holding rallies and making speeches. I could not understand their language, but some people obviously did understand it, because they stood there and listened to them.

The Polish nationalists despised the Soviet communists in spite of their apparent friendliness. The nationalists murdered two Soviet commissars. The Soviets issued a strict warning against such violence, and made it clear that dire consequences would result from such actions. A large funeral was held for the two murdered commissars and they were buried in the town square.

The Soviet forces, we found out, were waiting at the gates of Warsaw while the Luftwaffe bombed the city and its last remnants of resistance to shreds. Poland as we knew it was no more. The schools did not reopen and no one seemed to know what was going on.

To us children, it was like having an extended vacation. My parents, though, seemed very upset. I could tell by their hushed conversations and worried looks that things were not good at all. Every so often, some relative or friend dropped by and asked us what our plans for the future were. Events progressed fast, and with no reliable news it was very difficult to make rational decisions.

Our town had been occupied for about two weeks when the Soviets told everyone that they had orders to pull back to the Bug River, about fifteen miles east from Chelm. They offered transportation by train to anyone willing to leave with them. The Germans, they said, would occupy Chelm after they left. Later we found out that Hitler and Stalin had agreed to divide Poland between them. In return for their retreat to the Bug, the Soviets were to acquire the Baltic states of Lithuania, Latvia, and Estonia.

We knew that the Soviets meant business when they dug up the graves of the two murdered commissars and shipped them back to Russia. They told us the deadline for departure was October 4, 1939.

For my parents, this was a period of tremendous strain. There was heated debate about whether to go. What would my father do in the new land to make a living? How were we going to take our possessions on a packed train?

Grandmother Gitl was now living with her daughter Hendl, but what about Grandmother Naomi? The questions were endless and the answers few.

My parents had been married for thirteen years. They had saved up for a new apartment and for my education. Now it seemed like all their dreams were about to evaporate.

After much debate, it was decided that Papa and Wolf would take the train to Lubomel, my father's birthplace, about fifteen miles east of the Bug on what was now the Soviet side. My father used to get a Yiddish newspaper and he was constantly cursing Hitler, so perhaps what he already knew about the Germans contributed to his decision to tie our fate to the Soviets. Furthermore, all of my father's family was in Lubomel. One of his uncles raised and sold horses there. The plan was to send a team of horses with a wagon to bring us and Frieda, together with our belongings, to Lubomel.

Papa and Wolf left for Lubomel, and we settled down to pack. Mama did not have any suitcases, so all of our belongings were laid out neatly on large sheets and blankets. We tied together the four corners of the blankets, forming a satchel. Now we waited nervously for a wagon to take us to Lubomel. In the meantime, Frieda managed to find a one-horse cart in which she could make the journey. Our larger family needed a bigger wagon, but we could not find one locally that was willing to risk the trip. The journey was in fact very dangerous. In addition to the threat posed by robbers, unscrupulous drivers would sometimes abandon their passengers on the road, and occasionally a German plane would strafe the wagons.

The very idea of traveling in a wagon to another city was exciting to Moshe and me. Our anticipation overshadowed the inconvenience of living out of a packed bundle. I felt strange about my father being away from home. My mother took me aside and told me that I was now the man of the house. She entrusted me with our life savings: 1,500 Polish zloty in paper bills. She placed the money and some other valuables in a bag with a string, which she then tied around my neck and tucked inside my shirt. The responsibility made me feel very important. I told mother that I would guard it with all my cunning and strength. I needn't have worried much. In one month's time the Polish currency would be virtually worthless.

Grandmother Naomi agreed to move from her daughter Rachel's apartment into ours. The rent was paid up for the year, so she was to live there and use what we left behind. She did not wish to go with us. "If my fate is to die, I would rather die at home," she proclaimed. "I am too old to travel to God knows where, and I do not wish to be a burden on you, my children. You, my children, go—and may our Father in Heaven keep you under his wings and protect you!" To Moshe and me, she said: "You, my loved ones, are young, and the whole world out there is waiting for you. May you go in peace and may good fortune be with you all your days." Moshe and I told her that we would become doctors and come back to take the wrinkles out of her face. She smiled and said: "Have faith in God and remember the *Shema*: 'Hear, O Israel, the Lord our God, the Lord is one!'"

With a bit of luck, my father was able to find a driver. Three days after his departure from Chelm, a wagon arrived for us. We loaded it hurriedly, and with tears in our eyes we bid our last goodbyes to our grandmothers, aunts, uncles, and cousins. We left on the dirt road leading east towards the river Bug.

Three days later, on October 7, 1939, the Germans took over the city of Chelm. By November 6, 1942, the date of the last big transport of Jews from Chelm to the death camp at Sobibor, the Germans had murdered most of the city's Jewish population of over 15,000. Among the very few survivors of the camps from Chelm were my mother's sister Gitl and two of her children, Arie and Zelda. (I have never been able to learn the whole story of their terrible ordeal. I met Arie again years later in Israel. When I tried to speak to him about their experiences, he broke down in tears.)

Grandmother Naomi, as I mentioned earlier, was murdered by the SS. The same fate befell Naomi's daughter Rachel and Rachel's own daughters, Yenta and Shindel. Shindel had earlier been raped by a Gymnasium student. Rachel's son, Munish, was able to flee the Germans and escape to the U.S.S.R. with his father. There they were drafted into the Red Army, and both were later killed in combat.

In the end, the Germans had murdered my two grandmothers, six first cousins, two uncles, one aunt, and a large number of more distant relatives.

I began to feel homesick even before we left town. People waved farewell as we passed the familiar places. We rode past the Jewish cemetery where my grandfathers and several generations of my ancestors had been laid to rest. It had been in existence for five hundred years. In the distance I could see Koszcuiszko, and I wondered when I would be able to go back to school. The town began to fade in the distance, and we began to pass by unfamiliar farms and forests.

We encountered Soviet sentries who stopped us and asked if we had any firearms. When I showed them my blow-dart gun, they laughed and waved us on.

My homesickness eventually faded, and the excitement of the journey took over. Moshe and I began to chatter and play on top of the wagon. But when the driver stopped to adjust the harness, he asked us to get off and walk for a while to lighten the load on the horses.

The driver was Jewish, and a good friend of Papa's family in Lubomel. He told us that he had heard about robberies by bands of Polish army units hiding out in the forests. But he quickly calmed my mother's nerves by saying that this particular road was safe. The road itself was pockmarked with rain-filled bomb craters. Here and there we passed some dead horses, remnants of the Polish cavalry. The stench was awful and we held our noses. There were also some abandoned cars on the side of the road—victims of the gasoline shortage, or possibly of mechanical failure.

It was late afternoon when we reached the new border of the Soviet Union, the steel bridge that spanned the Bug. The Bug is a tributary to the larger Wistula, which crosses the city of Warsaw and empties into the Baltic Sea in the north. I was somewhat disappointed to see that the river bed was nearly dry, for I had expected it to be just as full as the Wistula. I had swum in the Wistula when we visited Aunt Luba and her family in 1937. The river was wide and its waters were swift. I ventured out past the markers and was caught by the current and dragged under. I knew how to swim, but I was not a strong swimmer. Luckily, a young man saw me bobbing and gasping for air, and he pulled me out by my trunks. It was a frightening experience. Ever since that day, I've felt a pang of fear when I go swimming and my feet leave the bottom.

The horses, encouraged by the driver, strained their muscles to pull the wagon onto the bridge over the Bug. Our wheels made a loud clatter rolling over the steel. Past the bridge was a Soviet checkpoint. The sentry stopped us and asked again if we had firearms. He looked over the wagon and offered me a chunk of Russian bread. Then he said: *Vam budyet khorosho v Sovyetskom Soyuze*—"You will fare well in the Soviet Union."

After we crossed the border my mother felt safer. The scenery had not changed much except that the sun had gone down and it was chilly. Soon the horses slowed and the driver had to urge them on with his whip. About eight miles from our destination one horse began to limp. The driver unhitched the good horse and rode into town to bring back a fresh team. He said it was not far and he would be back soon.

My mother must have been afraid being there alone with her two boys on a strange road in a strange land, but I was oblivious to her feelings. It took over three hours for the driver to return. First we heard the clatter of hooves in the dark and then we saw the outline of the horses and three men. As they came closer we recognized my father and uncle. We were overjoyed to see them. Papa and Wolf had been away for only three days, but to me it had seemed much longer.

When we arrived in Lubomel, all of our relatives came to greet us. We moved in with my mother's cousin, who lived in a three room house with a large, glassed-in porch. We bedded down on the floor in the dining room and before long I was fast asleep.

Early in the morning, I was awakened by my two young cousins urging Moshe and me to join them in the task of taking their horses to the pasture. What an adventure! Riding bareback on real horses was an opportunity we could not pass up. The only horse I had ever ridden was a stick, which I used when we played Cowboys and Indians. This was to be the real thing. We were so excited that we charged out to the stables without eating breakfast. Our cousins were seasoned riders, so we simply followed their lead. When we reached the stables each one of us selected a horse and climbed on. It didn't dawn on me that they would gallop. I simply assumed that they would walk to the pasture. But the horses were hungry, and the minute the gates were opened they charged out at full speed. Nothing could have stopped them.

I held on to my horse's mane for dear life. I was sliding from side to side and bouncing like a ping-pong ball. About halfway to the pasture I fell off, and then Moshe did too. We hit the dusty road bottom, got up, brushed ourselves off, and walked the rest of the way. Later, after a few more unsuccessful tries and some coaxing from my cousins, we managed to stay on our mounts.

David Goldman, our great uncle, owned the town's only bathhouse. Moshe and I used to hang out around the bathhouse with our cousins and watch the Soviet soldiers come in for showers or baths. On various occasions the soldiers let us take puffs of their *makhorka* cigarettes—a crude type of hand-rolled tobacco that was very coarse and burned the tongue. I tried it once and almost choked from coughing. The soldiers thought it was funny, but I learned my lesson and never took up smoking. Once, when the soldiers had undressed and gone in to take their showers, we rummaged through their clothing and stole some of their insignia so we could use them in our games.

It was in Lubomel that I began to feel hunger for the first time in my life. Our food was largely bread and some vegetables. Tea was abundant, so we drank lots of it. But it seemed impossible for me to get enough to eat.

Across the street from Uncle David's bathhouse lived my great aunt Judith Goldman and her only daughter Sosya. It was Sosya who inspired me to learn Russian. She was about seventeen at the time. She was a very pretty girl and was attending a formerly Polish school that had adopted the Soviet curriculum. Sosya told me that it was easy to make the transition from Polish to Russian. She showed me the Russian alphabet, which I memorized. Then she had me read from a Russian book. I could not understand all of it, but nevertheless I learned to read. Because Russian is a Slovak language, many of the words are similar to Polish. After a little practice I could speak some Russian and managed to talk to the Soviet soldiers.

I became fond of Judith and Sosya. They were good-natured people with few possessions. Most of their belongings had been sold in anticipation of their immigrating to the United States. Aunt Judith's husband Yitzhak Goldman had left some years earlier and was living in Brooklyn. Judith had had all of their papers processed, but could not get a medical clearance to emigrate because she had trachoma, an eye disease. To cure trachoma was a lengthy process without penicillin, which had not yet been discovered. While we were in Lubomel she finally received her medical clearance, but could not leave because of the war. Many years later I met Uncle Yitzhak in Brooklyn. In 1941 the Germans had overrun Lubomel and murdered all of my relatives, including Judith and Sosya.

Fall was in full swing. The trees were turning red and gold, and the nights were getting colder and longer. We moved in with Uncle David's family in order to relieve the burden of overcrowding at Mama's cousin's. Uncle David lived at 9 Ribna Street in a two room house. Their family and ours totaled ten people.

I could sense by my parents' behavior that our situation was grave. While my brother and I felt that we were on a kind of long vacation, my parents were filled with despair. Lubomel was a very small town and could not support many newcomers, much less the thousands of refugees who had poured in from the German side of the border.

The newest refugees brought with them tales of atrocities carried out by the Germans. Many of them lost their wives and children on the way. Among the refugees, there were some children who had lost their parents. The border at the Bug was now officially closed, and the Soviets were arresting—and sometimes shooting—anyone lucky enough to reach the east bank of the river.

My uncle Yitzhak Karp was one of those captured while crossing the river, and he was sent to Siberia. Yitzhak had married Grandma Gitl's daughter Hendl in 1937. He was in the dry goods business. One year later they had a little boy. As I mentioned earlier, Yitzhak had been able to elude the SS dragnet, but his wife, their baby, and Gitl were captured and sent to Sobibor, where they were gassed.

Refugees were everywhere in Lubomel. They slept in hallways, abandoned buildings, railway stations, and wherever they could find an empty spot. The bread lines were endless, and when one was lucky enough to find bread at all, it could be had only at an exorbitant price. The Polish currency was still in circulation, but it was highly inflated. The Soviet Army set up several soup lines to feed the people, but it was not enough.

With no reliable news, people clung to all sorts of rumors. One rumor was that the Germans would welcome any refugee willing to come back to occupied Poland. Some people tried their luck going back home. I believe that most of those who did so were Polish Catholics. Another rumor was that the

Soviets would welcome anyone willing to settle in the Soviet Union. Settling in the U.S.S.R., the State of the Proletariat, seemed to be the best option to most everyone.

Father found work doing odd jobs at a Soviet government building. About the same time, the authorities announced a call to exchange Polish currency for Soviet currency at the "official" rate. This exchange left my family with practically no money at all. My father was therefore happy to have a job, even though the pay was very low.

It was early November, 1939. We had been away from home a little over a month. I do not know how much longer we could have stayed at Uncle David's place, which was severely overcrowded. We were all getting in one another's way. But our worries seemingly came to an end with the declaration by the government office that all refugees were to register for resettlement in the U.S.S.R.

The registration desk was set up at the railway station. We gathered up our bundles and walked to the station to register and wait for transportation. Our relatives escorted us to bid us goodbye. The railway station was an old brick building with large double doors and windows. The ramp was elevated to the level of the freight car doors and constructed of rough boards that were almost black from age and weather.

My father picked out a spot near the main door, where we placed our bundles. Uncle Wolf and Aunt Frieda put their bundles next to ours. Moshe and I were assigned the task of watching the luggage. Within the hour, the entire area was swarming with refugees willing to register to be resettled in the Soviet Union. A uniformed official set up a registration desk with several clerks who began to process the refugees. Each registered group of thirty people was assigned to a rail car.

Our relatives stood by, giving us all kinds of advice and asking us to write to them. They also gave us some bread and dried fruit to take with us on our journey. We appreciated the gifts of food, for we knew that they did not have enough for themselves, much less enough to give away.

We were told that the train would be made up of freight cars, and would arrive by evening. But nightfall came and there was no train. Again the commissar showed up with an announcement that the train would be late, and that we should be ready to board it tomorrow. Some of the people stretched out on their luggage, made the best of it, and tried to sleep. With all the excitement, however, I did not want to sleep. I wanted to see and feel what it was like to stay up all night.

My parents urged me to go to sleep, but I was determined to stay awake. I grew dizzy, but did not give up. Dawn broke, and then I fell asleep on one of the bundles.

I was awakened by Moshe shouting "Get up! The train is here and we have to go!" My head was spinning. Moshe was pointing to a great snake of boxcars pulled by two locomotives. It was the longest train I had ever seen. Someone said it was a mile long.

When the train stopped, everybody rushed forward at once. There was much shouting. It was a scene of total pandemonium. As people identified their box car numbers, things calmed down a bit. Wolf and my father spotted our car and were the first ones on. The boxcar was outfitted with two levels of bunks, fashioned from rough boards. We were able to secure an upper bunk next to a window. In the center of the car floor was a hole to be used for a toilet. The space around the hole was partitioned off by a blanket for privacy. The box car had the markings P.K.P., *Polskie Koleje Painstwowe*—Polish Government Railways.

Our relatives came once again to wish us good luck. They told us to write. Although we would soon see them again, their fate was sealed by the fact that they felt no compulsion, as we did, to leave Lubomel. After all, it was their hometown. Just two years later, every last one of them would be murdered by the Germans.

It took several hours to load the train. Finally the locomotive released steam, and with a long, drawn-out whistle jerked the cars forward. We were on our way eastward. I watched our relatives through the little window until they looked like specks in the distance.

The first stop was the city of Kovel, about fifty kilometers from Lubomel. The commandant of the transport train checked the registration of all the refugees and appointed leaders for each boxcar. A leader's responsibility was to see to it that sanitary conditions were maintained in the car, and that food was distributed in an orderly manner.

My father was chosen to be the leader in our wagon. At appointed stations, his job was to bring in buckets of food and distribute measured portions to each person. Generally the portions consisted of a cup of soup and a slice of bread. Wolf and I helped my father bring the food to the car.

We remained in Kovel several hours, so my parents went to town to buy some provisions. They still had some Polish currency that they had not exchanged for rubles, so they decided to spend it while they could. As Kovel was a much larger city than Lubomel, there was much more food available in the open markets. They bought Polish sausage, bread, and some nonperishable foods at highly inflated prices, and returned to the train.

One of the families in our car produced a record player with a crank and some records, and entertained us with music and comedy. As the train rolled eastward, we passed many little farms with thatched roofs. When we arrived in the town of Dzolbunov, on the original Soviet border, we disembarked and were told that we would switch to another train. The Soviet railways were somewhat wider gauge than the Polish, so the two systems were not compatible.

The cars of the Soviet train had been cleaned and disinfected. They were also much wider and roomier that the Polish cars. After all of us were settled, we were registered again and issued portions of soup and black bread.

As our train crossed the old border of Poland, our car fell totally silent. I had a strange and inexplicable feeling upon entering this new country. Poland felt like home—the only home I had ever known. I knew nothing about this land called Ukraine. The adults talked a good deal about the proletarian state. According to the bits and pieces of conversation that I could understand, it was supposed to be a land of milk and honey. Everyone on our train seemed to be happy to be going to the Soviet Union. I did not understand it all.

Our first official welcome to the U.S.S.R. was given to us in the village Shepetovka. The village delegation, bearing red banners with inscription of welcome, greeted us at the rail station. Officials made speeches, which I could not understand except for the words *communisticheskaya* and *proletaryee*. The welcome party made us feel good, especially when little Ukrainian school girls, dressed in traditional garb, offered us hard candy that they carried in baskets. We were also fed at the station. Then we bid the welcome party thanks and goodbye, and with uplifted spirits departed to our unknown destination.

The train finally came to a small station where we were told to disembark and wait for trucks to take us wherever we were going. While we were waiting, some of the locals came by to look us over. They did not say much. When the flatbed trucks arrived, each group of families was assigned to a vehicle. Each truck was going to a different destination. As best as we could understand, our family, along with Wolf and Frieda, were going to a place called *zavod* or "factory." This *zavod* was a sugar-producing plant. The sugar plant and village was located near the town Guysin in the Vinnitsa district of the Ukrainian Republic. We had no idea where this was.

The trip was a bumpy one over an unpaved country road. All of us had to hold on to each other to keep from falling off the truck, as it was a flat bed with no guard rails. I thought the ride was fun—after all, it was my first one ever in a truck. But the women screamed with every bump and turn the vehicle made.

The truck had what looked like two hot-water tanks mounted on each side of the cab. One of the drivers kept feeding chunks of wood into the tanks to keep the fire going. The driver explained that the gas, a byproduct of the burning wood, was used to fuel the truck engine. I never did figure out the system, nor have I ever heard of such a thing since then.

A short while later we arrived at the *zavod* village. The sugar plant was a large red brick building with the tallest smokestack I had ever seen. The entire complex was surrounded by a high brick wall. It was a cold and overcast evening when we arrived. Even I was depressed, so I can only imagine how my parents felt. But after a short while, our morale received a boost when a factory delegation showed up with banners and placards welcoming us to their factory. They offered us more hard candy and invited us to the *Krasniy Ugolok* (Red Corner), a communist meeting hall.

At the meeting hall, a welcoming committee made some more speeches and then took us to our living quarters. Our family and Wolf and Frieda received one large room in a two-story building. The room had a high ceiling and wooden floors. The furniture consisted of six iron beds, a wooden table with two benches, and a wood-burning stove for heating and cooking. Water was drawn from a well outside. The outhouse was communal and was used by all the tenants of the building. We divided the room between our families and settled down as best as we could. Papa and Wolf were given a couple of days to rest and familiarize themselves with the area. After that, they were to begin their employment at the sugar plant.

Chapter Three

In the Ukraine

In the morning Moshe and I went outside to explore the village. The entire village, we discovered, consisted of a single street lined with cottages and two-story apartment buildings that belonged to the plant and housed its workers. The surrounding countryside was hilly and rather picturesque. A short distance from our apartment and down a hill was a fairly large lake surrounded by mature trees.

The plant itself was a great brick structure with a smokestack that belched smoke far into the sky. With its high wall, the plant resembled a prison more than a sugar factory. It reminded me of the Paviak prison I had seen when we visited Aunt Luba in Warsaw in 1937.

Moshe and I soon met our neighbors, a boy and girl our age, and we hit it off with them right away. Even though we could not communicate very well, we managed to play together. They showed us their schoolbooks and gave us a short lesson in the Russian language.

Our neighbors raised chickens and pigs in the back yard. Once when Moshe and I were visiting our new playmates, their father slaughtered a pig. He knocked the pig unconscious, and then cut its throat with a long knife. On several occasions the neighbors also invited Moshe and me to a dinner of boiled chicken and potatoes, which we ate with great zeal.

We were very happy to accept these invitations, for food was rationed in our new village. Surprisingly, however, we refugees enjoyed certain privileges, including going to the front of any food line. This did not endear us to the locals. Moshe and I were nevertheless always hungry, as the rations were never enough to feed us all.

My parents did not like our new situation. Papa and Wolf (who was a tailor by trade) had worked at the same jobs their whole lives. Their new employment, shoveling and sorting sugar beets, was not what they had in mind when they came to the Soviet Union. They could not see any future in this place. They therefore decided to travel to the town of Guysin, about fifty kilometers away, to seek new jobs and lodging for the family. But they had to employ great secrecy in doing so, because the NKVD—the People's Commissariat for Internal Affairs that sent so many millions of poor souls to the forced labor camps of the Gulag —had to approve any changes in residency or employment.

In Guysin, Papa found a Jewish man by the name of Shultz who happened to be the manager of a shoe cooperative. Wolf also found a tailoring cooperative. Both of them were accepted for work. To receive a permit to relocate to Guysin, however, they had to get permission from the office of the NKVD in Vinnitsa. Once Papa and Wolf established that they had jobs and places to live, the Vinnitsa office agreed to the relocation. But we also needed a permit from the local authorities to move out of the *zavod* village, and we were worried that they would refuse to grant one. So we did not seek their permission. Instead we packed our belongings and sneaked away in the middle of the night to catch the train to Guysin. My parents would not let me say goodbye to my friends, for fear of attracting the attention of the authorities.

We left for Guysin in December of 1939. We had been in Russia only about one month and away from home just a little over two months, but there had been so many changes in our lives that it seemed like years. The cold weather did not make matters any easier for us.

Guysin was a town of about 20,000 souls, roughly fifty kilometers southeast of Vinnitsa and one hundred and fifty kilometers south of Kiev, the capitol of the Ukraine. The southern River Bug (not the same one as in Poland) ran through the town and emptied into the Black Sea.

We arrived in Guysin in the morning and walked to the apartment of Mr. Shultz. The Shultzes were one of the few Jewish families in town. They were gracious enough to let us stay with them until we found a place of our own. Theirs was a small two-room apartment where they lived with their two teenagers, a boy and a girl who attended high school. We bedded down for the night on the dining-room floor next to a large glass-enclosed cabinet that contained their family china. The china, they told us, was over a hundred years old. The walls were decorated with several heirloom paintings from Warsaw.

We spent three days with the Shultzes. First we went to various government offices to receive rations and register, and then my parents set out to find a place to live. They soon found a red brick duplex on the edge of town. Meanwhile, Uncle Wolf and Aunt Frieda found their own apartment elsewhere in Guysin.

One side of our duplex was occupied by an old Ukrainian woman and a teenage girl. The other side was vacant. The building belonged to a nearby alcohol-producing plant, and, as a general rule, only employees of the alcohol plant were entitled to live in that particular building. When my parents told the city registrar about the empty apartment, however, the registrar advised us to move in. This was soon to produce unpleasant consequences for us.

My mother set up housekeeping and cleaned the apartment thoroughly. The main room was about fifteen by twenty feet, as was the kitchen, which had a large oven for heating and cooking. The furniture consisted of two iron beds, a table, and four chairs. The backyard was overgrown with dead weeds from the summer. On the edge of the yard was a broken-down clothesline, as well as an outhouse with weathered and rotting boards that were hanging loose from the frame. The street in front of the house was unpaved, and covered with sand and silt deposits left by the river when it flooded.

Moshe and I were registered to go to school, and our parents were assigned to evening courses to learn to read and write Russian. Because of the differences in language and curriculum, the school principal felt it best for us to start one grade behind, so I was put in the fifth grade and Moshe in the third. Ours was the only public school in Guysin. It consisted of six long barracks, and it was located at the opposite end of town. There was no transportation, so we walked to and from school regardless of the weather.

Luckily for me, students in the fifth and sixth grades could choose a program taught largely in Yiddish (the language we spoke at home) and staffed only by Jewish teachers. The other grades did not have that choice. My fifth grade curriculum included Yiddish language and literature, Russian grammar and literature, advanced Arithmetic, beginning Geometry, History, Geography, and Political Science. Part of the latter course included a section called *voyennoe delo*, or military training. We learned to handle the standard Soviet combat rifle and mock hand-grenades, and to pass secret messages through "enemy" lines. We also learned to administer first aid to the wounded. At the conclusion of our training we were awarded medals called G.O.S., *Gotov k Oboronye S.S.S.R.* — "Ready to Defend the Soviet Union."

All schoolchildren were also systematically drafted into the Pioneer youth movement, the forerunner of the Comsomol (a youth organization that led up to membership in the Communist Party). At the swearing-in ceremony for the Pioneers, I was given a red scarf and a special ring to bind it around my neck. The G.O.S. medal gave me a sense of achievement, and joining the Pioneers made me feel as if the other students and I shared a common bond. And indeed, in this communist country I experienced no religious discrimination and no name-calling. What a drastic change from the Polish schools! In spite of my constant hunger, I started to feel good about this new country.

I progressed fairly well in my studies, considering that I had to make up for four months of missed school and to study more advanced mathematics than

I had been prepared for in Poland. My math teacher lived nearby, and his daughter, who was in my class, helped me with my homework. Another classmate of mine, Reznitskaya, lived across the street from us and helped me with my Russian. Needless to say, I also benefited from the fact that many of the subjects were taught in Yiddish.

Yiddish was written somewhat differently in Russia than in Poland. In both countries, we utilized the Hebrew alphabet to write Yiddish words. In Hebrew, five of the letters—ב, מ, נ, פ, and צ—have a different shape when they occur at the end of a word, as follows: ך, ם, ן, ף, and ץ. In Poland we used these different letters when writing Yiddish, but in the Soviet Union we did not. I preferred the Soviet way, because I have never been able to discern any practical reason for the existence of these letters. The sound of the word is the same either way.

These differences do not matter much today, because after 1945 the Soviets eliminated Yiddish from the curriculum.

While I was settling into school, a rather serious problem was brewing for my family. The housing administrator of the alcohol plant found out about our moving into "his" housing unit, so he came by to pay us a visit. In no uncertain terms, he told us to move out, and he gave us a two week deadline. My parents pleaded with him to give us an extension at least until spring, when the weather would be warmer. It was still winter and it was freezing outside, which made it difficult for us to go looking for apartments. The administrator would not hear of it. "Two weeks is all you have!" he warned.

Two weeks later, however, we were still in the apartment. The administrator began to threaten eviction. Meanwhile, we were busily looking for a place to rent, but we could not find anything.

Then a local Russian Jew—a friend of ours named Haskel—had an inspired idea. He suggested that we appeal to the Supreme Soviet Chairman, Yosif Vissaryonovitch Stalin. He also suggested that *I* write the letter, and that I do so in my own childish handwriting.

Haskel offered to dictate the letter, so this is what I wrote:

"Dear Comrade Stalin: I am a twelve-year-old refugee from Poland who has recently come to the Soviet Union with my parents and settled in the city of Guysin in the region of Vinnitsa. The administrator of the local alcohol plant is going to evict us from our apartment. We cannot find another apartment in town. Please help us if you can."

I signed the letter and wrote down our address.

Two more weeks passed, and we heard nothing. Papa talked to his boss and asked him if he could intervene, but he could not help us. The threat of eviction loomed large.

Then, out of the blue, a uniformed officer came to see us. The officer asked about our situation and took notes on a pad. At first we thought he was going to evict us, and my mother began to cry. But then the commissar told us that he had been sent from Chairman Stalin's office to investigate the matter. He told us not to worry: the plant administrator would not bother us again. He then asked me if it was I who had written the letter. When I said that it was, he put his hand on my shoulder and said with a smile "*Khoroshey molodyets!* (Fine lad!) You can stay here as long as you like."

Several days later the housing administrator came by to apologize. He reaffirmed that we could stay in the house, and he even offered my father a job in the alcohol plant. One can only imagine what kind of pressure had been put on him to make him change his tune so completely.

The winter of 1939–1940 was cold and seemed very harsh to me. I had outgrown the warm coat I brought from Poland, and I was undernourished. We had no wood for heating the apartment, so we burned old papers and dry weeds to keep warm. Our meager rations of flour and grain did not go far, and we always ran out before the next allotment of food. Mama tried to stretch the food as far as she could, but it was never enough. She spent most of her time looking for stores that might have a little bread for sale, and standing in long lines when she found some. Mama showed me how to patch the torn places on my winter coat to make it last longer. For socks we substituted newspapers, which we used to wrap our feet. There were no clothing stores, which didn't matter anyway because we had no money to spend on clothes.

War had broken out between the U.S.S.R. and Finland at the very end of November 1939. It was a harsh war for both sides, as it was fought in very cold weather. As I understand it, the war became a testing ground for the Axis powers to evaluate the capability and equipment of the Soviets in preparation for the big battles to come. I saw army units from Guysin march to the rail station, on their way to fight the Finns.

Shortages of food and other goods became increasingly acute because of the war in Finland. Mama literally spent whole days standing in line for bread. Quite often, all of the available bread was gone when she finally reached the counter. Then she would have to find another bread line and start all over again. Moshe and I scoured the countryside for dead trees or branches to keep the apartment warm and heat the stove for cooking. Afflicted as we were by cold and hunger, it was very difficult for us to do our homework. In spite of it all, we were still occasionally able to skate and even to ski.

There was not much socializing or entertainment that winter in Guysin. Once in a while Moshe and I would go to propaganda movies, depicting the battles of the Heroic Communist Revolution. I participated in some plays that were organized by the local Pioneers and held in the Red Corner.

As you can imagine, my parents were very unhappy with our situation. Guysin had about a dozen or so families of Polish Jews listed as refugees. The

NKVD kept us under constant surveillance and repeatedly required us to register at their offices. Every time my parents registered, they were issued new identification papers.

During one of those registrations, we refugees were informed that orders from "higher up" required us to move to another city. We were told that we could not stay in Guysin for reasons of state security. We were to move to Uman, about 150 kilometers from Vinnitsa. Perhaps because Uman rhymes with Haman, the villain in the Book of Esther, none of the refugees were eager to move.

We told the NKVD Chief that we liked Guysin and wanted to stay. After about two months, another meeting was called. This time, the NKVD said that we had a choice: we could move voluntarily or be resettled by force.

Our situation was one of near starvation, and we faced yet another move. This was one of many times we longed for our home.

My parents then made a fateful decision: we would try to return to Poland. By bribing an acquaintance who happened to be a train conductor, my father was able to secure passage to Poland for us as well as Wolf and Frieda.

It was now the spring of 1940. The ice on the river was breaking up, creating jams around bridges and sharp bends. This caused the river to spill over its banks and into the low areas of the city. Army sappers were busy blowing up the ice jams, but this did not seem to alleviate the flooding. Our street was cut off because of the rising water, and our house, which was situated on a small mound of land, looked like an island.

It was during these floods that we packed our belongings and waded through the street to the railroad station. Once again we left at night without saying goodbye to our friends, and with one eye out for the NKVD.

The small rail station was packed with travelers, and it seemed that there would not be enough space on the train to accommodate all of us. To our surprise, the train was of the "midget" variety. The passenger cars were not much taller than me, and the locomotive looked like it belonged in an amusement park. I asked one of the passengers why the cars were so small. He told me that the train had belonged to a wealthy landowner, and had been seized as state property at the time of the Russian Revolution.

When the train pulled into the station, everyone scrambled at once in an effort to board it. In the process I became separated from my family. The mass of people surging forward literally swept me off the ground and carried me and my bundle into the car. Moshe went through the same experience. Inside the car we were in total darkness, as the windows were completely covered up by all of the bodies pressed against them. Finally I heard my mother's call, and Moshe and I shouted back so she would know that we had all made it on board.

The little train started out very slowly, huffing and puffing at a snail's pace into the dark countryside. I fell asleep standing up, but there was no danger that I would fall to the floor because I was propped up by the crush of people around me.

I was awakened by a commotion and noticed the gray light of dawn filtering into the car. It took me a while to get my bearings. I then realized that the train had stopped, and that my mother was calling me to get off. We had arrived in Vinnitsa.

In 1926 there were almost 22,000 Jews in Vinnitsa—roughly 40% of the city's total population. When we went through the town in 1940, the Jewish population must have been somewhat larger than that. But on September 22, 1941—the Jewish holy day of Rosh Hashanah—the Germans murdered 28,000 Jews from Vinnitsa and the surrounding villages.[1]

I wanted to visit the city, but circumstances were not in my favor. We were obliged to settle down in the stationhouse to wait for the train to Kiev, the capitol of the Ukraine.

Inside the station was a small restaurant that was completely empty. Moshe and I went into the restaurant to try our luck at finding some food. There was no food being served, but I did find hot mustard on the tables. I had never had mustard, so I tasted a spoonful of it. Needless to say, I was immediately sorry I had done so. I ran outside gagging and spitting, and my mouth felt as if it was on fire. Moshe was right behind me, not knowing whether to laugh or cry. It was a hard lesson that I would not forget.

I was still hungry when the train to Kiev arrived. This time the passenger cars were the regular size. Moshe and I settled down next to a window on a hardwood bench.

Kiev was about two hundred kilometers away. As we approached the city, the rails branched out into multiple tracks and the train traffic became heavier. The buildings looked bigger than in other towns, and there were many more of them. With its trams and electric buses, Kiev reminded me of Warsaw.

The train finally slowed down and came to a stop in front of the main terminal building. It was a huge building with many ramps leading to various trains departing for many different destinations. There were swarms of people rushing in every direction.

We disembarked and followed the crowd to the main terminal. When we arrived, we were surprised to see that the terminal lobby was crammed with families of refugees just like us, spread out all over the floor and sitting on their bundles. All these people were attempting to go back to Poland, just as we were. Some of them, we learned later, had been waiting for a train for several weeks.

Kiev is situated on the Dnieper River, which flows into the Black Sea, and so lies at the crossroads between Western Europe, the Orient, and the Middle East. Given its advantageous location, it is not surprising that Jews had inhabited the city since the time of its founding in the 8th century. Although the Jewish community of Kiev was subject to pogroms and other misfortunes over the centuries, it continued to grow. By 1939, the city's Jewish population had expanded to 175,000.[2] This number was never to be exceeded. On September 29–30, 1941, little more than a week after the Germans marched into Kiev, thousands of the city's Jewish families were ordered to appear at Babi Yar, a ravine in the suburbs. There they were machine-gunned by the SS, with the help of a Ukrainian militia. But the killing did not stop there. After the war, more than 100,000 corpses were discovered at Babi Yar. Most of them were Jews.

When I look back, it is hard to believe what was happening at that train station in Kiev. There we were, waiting with hundreds of other Jewish refugees for a chance to return to Poland—where the Germans would happily have herded us into the gas chambers of the death camps.

I have no explanation for why all those refugees simultaneously chose to return to Poland. In any case, I suspect that the NKVD was not displeased by this turn of events. After all, we had been prompted to leave Guysin by the NKVD's threat of forced resettlement, and I doubt that all the refugees could have escaped the notice of the authorities while traveling hundreds of miles without permits. But what did these people imagine they would find in Nazi-occupied Poland?

I wish I had thought to ask my parents what exactly they had in mind. But I doubt they really knew the answer.

We managed to find a spot on the tile floor of the terminal lobby to lay down our bundles and wait for the next train to Poland. After we settled down, Moshe and I ventured out to explore the area in search of food. It did not take us long to find out that we refugees were confined to the main hall. All the rest of the station was out of bounds to us. But Moshe and I ignored this restriction.

The interior of the station, we discovered, was magnificently decorated with statues and sculptures commemorating figures of the great Proletarian Revolution. The grandeur of the design, which included immense chandeliers hanging from the ceiling, was awesome. We had never seen anything like it. It was as if we were visiting a museum.

Soon we found a small restaurant where the smell of cooked food made my stomach growl. Moshe and I casually walked in. The waiters were busy serving food to uniformed men and officials. Some of the people gave us suspicious looks, and before long a man came over and told us to get out.

As we walked out of the restaurant, I told Moshe that we should grab some bread off the tables, split up, and run. Several moments later we were lost in the crowd with bread in our hands. Moshe and I devoured the stolen food without saying a word to each other.

When I told my mother about our adventure, she screamed at us never to do any such thing ever again. Yet she did not punish us, probably because she was just as hungry as we were.

Papa and Wolf somehow found a way into town, in spite of the fact that the police were guarding the station exits. They came back with bread and some other food. Mama rationed out the food so that it would last as long as possible. This turned out to be a good idea, because we were to spend about a week to ten days in that railroad station.

I soon met a boy my age, and he and Moshe and I sneaked into town together more than once. We would crawl through a broken fence and then hitch a ride on a tram. It was easier for us kids to get out of the station than for my parents, so my parents gave me some money to buy whatever food I might find. Bread was fairly easy to come by in Kiev, because it was not rationed as in Guysin.

Once we came across some schoolchildren on their way to a picnic. We stopped to talk to them and they invited us to join them. The picnic was in the municipal park and there was enough food to feed an army. The three of us ate until we were full. We were having a good time until an official came by and asked us for our tickets. I told him that the schoolchildren had the tickets and that we had come with them. Moshe and the other boy had overheard the conversation, so they slowly walked over to the fence that surrounded the park, then climbed over it and jumped down to the street. When the official turned in their direction and blew his whistle, I took off. We kept running until we reached the train station.

More and more refugees arrived with every passing day. Soon every inch of space in the terminal lobby was occupied. There must have been several hundred families in the lobby by the time we were able to leave.

One morning a uniformed official announced that a train was being formed to take us back to Poland. We were instructed to line up to register for the journey. After the registration we were told to board the train, which was waiting on a reserve track.

As we walked to the waiting train, my parents met several families whom they knew from back home. Their experiences in the Soviet Union were similar to ours, which is why they, too, had decided to return to Poland.

It took several hours to register all the people and fill up the train. Finally we departed. When we reached the little border town of Sarna, we disembarked in order to transfer to a train that could run on Poland's narrow tracks.

The next train to occupied Poland, we were told, would arrive the following day. My parents went into town to buy some food, but came back empty handed. We had to be satisfied with the little bread we had brought with us from Kiev.

In the morning the train arrived and we left Sarna for Lubomel, from which we had departed only six months before. As we traveled, I thought about school and wondered when I would ever catch up. In Guysin I had managed to attend only four months of the fifth grade.

We got as far as the city of Kovel, about fifty kilometers from Lubomel, when we were told to disembark. The train, we were informed, would go no further. We picked up our bundles and walked towards town. Mama wiped the tears from her eyes. When I asked her why she was crying, she managed a weak smile and said "Oh, it's nothing." She didn't want to alarm me by pointing out that we were facing nightfall in a strange city with no place to go and very little money.

The bright lights of the city and the people strolling up and down the street nonetheless gave Kovel a festive look. At one point, we came upon a store with wide stairs leading up to a locked door. My father decided that this was as good a place as any to spend the night. In the morning, he said, we would find a way to continue on to Lubomel.

As we were getting settled, someone called my parents' names. It was a friend whom we had not seen since the outbreak of the war. When he heard of our plight, he insisted that all of us—including Wolf and Frieda—spend the night in his apartment, where he lived with his wife.

Our friend's apartment was small and shabby. His wife was surprised to see us, but she welcomed us graciously and prepared a tasty meal that I gulped down immediately.

Moshe and I spread out on our bundles and fell asleep at once, while the adults sat at the table talking of their fears and hopes. We awoke in the morning to the smell of fried eggs, which our host served us for breakfast along with bread and tea. What a treat!—for we had not even seen eggs, much less eaten them, in six months.

We found out that our friends had been able to avoid resettlement in the interior of the U.S.S.R. They left Chelm when the Soviets withdrew across the Bug River, and had chosen to stop in Kovel. Things were rough for them, but they were able to get by, doing a little work and selling off some of the goods that they had brought with them from Chelm. We also learned that some of the refugees who had gone into the Soviet Union, as we did, came back immediately after experiencing the hardships there. This forewarned the other refugees to stay put.

We soon discovered that there were actually a good number of refugees from Chelm in Kovel, including one of my mother's cousins. We got in touch with this cousin, and she told us that that my father's cousins Hendl, Judith, and Mordechai had settled near the Ural Mountains in a place called Asbest. There they were supposedly working in the mines, quarrying asbestos rock — a frightful prospect, it seemed to us.

Our cousin insisted that we move in with her until we got ready to travel to Lubomel. We were happy to accept this kind offer.

Our cousin's husband supplied cattle to the slaughter house and was involved in the distribution of meat, so we had plenty of meat to eat while we stayed with them. But they also had their share of problems. In their effort to "communize" this newly conquered territory, the Soviets revised the existing economic system in such a way that incentives were lost, production suffered, and there were shortages of many necessary goods. In general, conditions in town were not much better than we had encountered in the Ukraine, and refugees were everywhere.

We were advised not to try to return to Chelm without getting rid of all evidence of our having been in the U.S.S.R. I was obliged to destroy my G.O.S. medal and Pioneer scarf and ring. At first I refused to do it, but in the end I gave in.

While in Kovel, I happened to meet my old friend David Nankin and his mother. David's mother was doing laundry for other people. Theirs was a hard lot, and I felt sorry for them. David had not attended school since the outbreak of the war in 1939. He was withdrawn and did not talk much. After that I never saw him again.

We stayed with our cousin until Papa and Wolf returned from Lubomel, where they had gone to see whether it was safe to return. The conditions in Lubomel were not much better than in Kovel, but at least we had more relatives there. I suppose, too, that my father felt a certain bond to his home town.

We finally caught a train to Lubomel, and after a short journey we arrived at the same station from which we had left six months before. We now learned that we were stuck: we were forbidden to cross the Bug.

Once again, we moved in with a cousin of my mother's. Wolf and Frieda moved in with another relative. My father found a job clearing land for a Russian army base. It didn't pay much, but it helped buy some food. Now there at last seemed to be enough to eat. I recall eating mostly bread, eggs, and sour cream, and drinking a lot of tea.

Refugees returning from the Ukraine kept coming into Lubomel every day, so that it seemed as if there were more refugees than local residents. Some of the refugees tried to cross the Bug illegally. Most of these were caught by Soviet border guards and sent to work camps in Siberia. Some refugees organized demonstrations demanding that they be allowed to go back "home." It was obvious that these protesters did not know much about the Soviets.

Demonstrations were unheard of in the U.S.S.R., and the authorities were not inclined to tolerate such outbursts.

One day, the authorities in Lubomel issued an order for all nonresidents to report for registration. Any nonresident who did not register, they said, would be subject to arrest. Rumors started to swirl among the refugees. Some said that we would be sent back into the interior of the U.S.S.R., while others said that we would be sent back to Nazi-occupied Poland.

I later found out that the Soviets had attempted to get the Germans to take back the Polish refugees who had crossed over into Soviet territory. Luckily for us, the Germans refused to accept the Polish refugees. To alleviate their refugee problem, the Soviets had to take other measures.

Just about everybody we knew registered. It turns out that this was all part of a master plan to deal with the Polish refugees by arresting them and shipping them into the interior of the U.S.S.R. The first to be shipped out were unmarried individuals. These unfortunate people, who had been arrested starting in February of 1940, were sent to the prison camps of the Gulag. Next, in March, married couples without children were rounded up. The last wave of arrests, in which married couples with children were apprehended (including, of course, my family), occurred in May and June. Unlike those in the first wave of arrests, these last two groups of refugees were lucky enough to be sent to villages in Siberia. There they were made to do exhausting and often dangerous work such as logging.

According to Polish estimates, between 1.5 and 1.7 million Poles were arrested in these three waves and forcibly resettled in the interior of the Soviet Union. 500,000 of these were Jews.[3] Who can guess how may of these Polish citizens perished under the harsh conditions to which they were exposed in the Gulag and in Siberia?[4]

About two weeks after we registered, our family was awakened one night by loud shouts and pounding on the door. When the door was opened, police, NKVD officials, and soldiers with rifles and bayonets burst in and demanded to know where the Goldman family was. They checked our cousin's residence papers, and told us to pack only what we could carry and no more. We were given only a few minutes in which to do so.

Mama began to cry, and so did Moshe. We could hear shouts and cries from the neighbor's house.

Outside in the gray dawn, we were herded into a group and taken to a waiting truck. Armed guards then escorted us to the railroad station. The entire station was cordoned off by police and armed soldiers. We were ordered off the truck and into the cordoned area.

It was still dark outside and we could not tell just how many people were there, but from the sounds of crying and the shouts of farewell it sounded like a large crowd. As the sun came up, we found Uncle Wolf and Aunt Frieda. By some chance, they had not been deported earlier along with the rest of the childless married couples.

We asked one of the Russian guards where they were taking us. *Vy yedete domoy*, he replied sardonically—"You are going home."

Our relatives came by to see what was happening. They could only stand there helplessly. The guards would not let them pass the cordon. Later, some of our relatives persuaded one of the guards to hand over some food for us to take along.

Before long, the train, made up of a string of box cars, pulled in. We were ordered to board. By now, we were experienced at finding the best spot in the car. This time, however, we were accompanied by armed guards, and they packed sixty people into each car. The car was much like the one in which we had first journeyed from Lubomel to the Ukraine. There were two long shelves on each side of it, with a long, narrow window above the top shelves. But this time, the windows were covered with barbed wire. And when the boxcar was full, a guard was posted on each end of it and the door was locked from the outside.

After the cars were locked, our relatives were permitted to come close so that they could talk with us. They also brought us bread and some fresh strawberries, the remains of the Sabbath meal that we never got to eat.

It was May of 1940.

That was the last time we saw our relatives. One year later, the Germans overran Lubomel. Not a single relative of ours from Lubomel survived the Holocaust. The Germans murdered them all.

NOTES

1. *Encyclopedia Judaica* (Jerusalem: Keter Publishing, 1971), vol. 16, 159, *s.v.* "Vinnitsa."

2. *Encyclopedia Judaica*, vol. 10, 995, *s.v.* "Kiev."

3. Henrik Greenberg, *Children of Zion* (in Hebrew), trans. from the original Polish by Zev Shos (Jerusalem: Grafit, 1995), 15.

4. According to Greenberg, it was reported to Stalin in 1944 that 389,382 Poles were at that time in exile or prison in the U.S.S.R. (*Children of Zion*, 15). If the Polish estimates of the numbers arrested in 1940 are accurate (which is of course uncertain), this may give us a rough idea of how many Poles must have died in the period since 1940.

Chapter Four

Siberia

We had no idea where we were going to be taken, but we did not really believe that the Soviets would send us back to Poland. I marked the eastern wall of our boxcar and said to my father: "If the locomotive is hooked up on the east side of the train, we will be going back to the Soviet Union."

The occupants of our car were mostly married couples and children. It was a mixed crowd of Polish Jews from all walks of life and from many different towns. There were no Polish Catholics in our car, but it turned out that there were many in the other boxcars.

A telephone line had been installed that ran all the way from the locomotive to the train's caboose. A car "captain" was appointed, and he submitted to the guards a head count of the people in his boxcar. When all the arrangements were concluded, the guards shut the car doors from the outside. This was to be the routine after every stop.

In the late afternoon of the day after we had been arrested, the train finally began to move. It was headed east. Only a few weeks after our return from the Soviet Union, we were being taken back into Mother Russia. Our fate was carrying us away from certain destruction by the Germans, but also toward unimagined misery.

Although many hardships lay ahead for us, we were in fact very fortunate. Had we moved to Uman in the Ukraine as we were ordered to do by the NKVD, or had we stayed in Lubomel, or had the Germans agreed to take back the Polish refugees from the U.S.S.R., my family and I would almost certainly have been murdered by the SS mobile killing-squads or sent to a death camp. That was the virtually inevitable fate of the Jews who remained in Poland, or who got caught up in the German invasion of the western part of the Soviet Union in 1941.

Our first stop was Kovel, which we had recently left. The boxcar doors were opened for a roll call and food. The food was delivered to us by the car captain—my father. Papa picked up the soup in buckets at the station terminal, and portioned out about a pint to each person. The watery soup and a slice of bread were supposed to sustain us from meal to meal. On a good day we would have three meals, but sometimes we had only one.

Someone found a long stick at one of the stops and succeeded in hiding it in the car. When the train was in motion, we poked the stick through the window and used it to unlatch the door. One of the guards cursed us when he saw the open door, and subsequently put a bolt through the latch. With perseverance and stubbornness, however, we overcame that obstacle as well: we used the stick as a hook to unbolt the latch. The guard screamed at us and threatened us, but he could not figure out how we managed to open the door. Finally he gave up and let us keep the door open, especially as we moved deeper into Soviet territory.

At times we lost all sense of direction and could not tell whether we were moving east or west. As we passed through towns and villages, we could sometimes see the residents turning their faces towards our train of human cargo with its locked doors, and shaking their heads in silent sorrow.

The guards introduced us to some new expressions. When the train was ready to move, they would shout the long, drawn-out order: *PO VAAHOWWNAAAM!* —On the Waaaagons! The other new term was *Spyets-Pereselentsy*—"Special Resettlers," meaning us. We were to hear these words frequently in the weeks and months ahead.

As we pushed deeper into the Soviet Union, the guards relaxed their vigilance, and we were permitted to get out of the cars and walk around the train. At such times, however, they surrounded the train, and we were not allowed to have any contact with local residents. Along the route, designated stations were to have soup and bread ready for us. But if the train was late or rerouted, we were not fed. Instead, we received *kipyatok*—hot water that smelled and tasted like locomotive steam.

Sometimes the train passed through restricted territory. On those occasions, the guards ordered the windows and doors shut. (And they meant it: they fired warning shots whenever an order was disobeyed.) During such periods we sat in the dark, and the stale air became unbearably hot. Some people fainted. A few cars down from us, an elderly doctor committed suicide.

The guards also introduced us to the most juicy Russian curses. When they began to curse, they could go on for several minutes without stopping.

Sometimes the guards allowed us to buy food from the locals to diversify our diet of soup. Four men once took advantage of this liberty, and went for a swim in a nearby river. The guards caught up with them and dragged them back to the train. They were incarcerated in the jail car for two days.

As our journey stretched into weeks, we gradually lost track of the number of days we had been underway. Instead, places became points of temporal reference, so that we would say "when we were in Kursk," or "when we were in Sverdlovsk."

Once in a while, our train stopped at a *razyezd* or siding to let other trains pass. Then one could sometimes see trainloads of prisoners passing by. Their boxcars were similar to ours, except that the doors were bolted shut and they had bars on their windows as well as barbed wire.

East, east, east we went, the clickety-clack of the wheels on the track as endless as the horizon. When we pulled into Sverdlovsk, a large industrial city at the gates of the Ural Mountains that separate Europe from Asia, our train was parked on a side track and we were locked inside for twenty-four hours with no explanation. The following day, however, the heads of each family received permission to go into town. Papa and Wolf set out to buy some provisions. In town, Papa met some other Polish refugees who had received temporary Soviet citizenship and had come to Sverdlovsk through a refugee resettlement program similar to the one that took us to the Ukraine. They were lucky to have been assigned to a large city, and they were apparently not harassed by the NKVD as we were in Guysin.

While in Sverdlovsk, we received a lumpy cereal and plenty of bread in addition to the daily soup. The cereal was filling and tasted good.

Before our departure from Sverdlovsk, eight boxcars full of refugees were disconnected from our train and sent, as we later found out, to the city of Asbest. Asbest was a mining town where raw material was extracted from the earth for the production of asbestos. (The Soviets had pragmatically named the town after the mineral.) The mining was carried out manually, and with no protection against deadly dust. Many people died after just several months in the mine shafts. Several years later I found out that Papa's cousins Mordechai, Hendl and Judith, who were sent to Asbest, cleverly played sick from the beginning and were given different jobs. Thus they escaped the virtual certainty of lung disease.

By the time we left Sverdlovsk, sixty of us had been living in our boxcar for three weeks. All of us were filthy. We tried to wash up whenever possible, but could almost never manage to clean more than our faces and hands. On rare occasions, we were able to strip to the waist and wash our upper bodies. But we had no soap, and there was no way to clean our clothes. Some people were suffering from malnutrition and had sores from vitamin deficiencies. All of us had lice in our clothing and hair.

In spite of our misery, we also had moments of joy. The scenery in the Ural Mountains was absolutely breathtaking. I had never seen snow-capped peaks before. The mountains seemed to hover over us, dwarfing the train and everything else around us. Every so often, we crossed rushing streams and wide rivers. The intensely green vegetation enhanced the virgin beauty of the countryside.

As we crossed the Urals, our train descended into the Siberian plain. On both sides of us were forests of pine and birch.

About two days after leaving Sverdlovsk, we came to the city of Omsk. Omsk lies on the southwestern edge of Siberia, and was known during the era of the tsars as the city of exile. Jewish children who were seized for military service were sent to the Cantonist Regiment in Omsk. The Jewish community in Omsk was accordingly formed by men who had served in the tsar's army.

In Omsk we received some tasty soup, which had some meat in it for a change. I did not know what kind of meat it was, and I did not care; the soup tasted very good, and that is all that mattered. Maybe some of the Jews of Omsk helped to provide this meal for us.

As we left Omsk, I was able to get a better view of the city. As far as I could tell, most of it was made up of log cabins and low houses spread out in an irregular pattern. The city looked dull and gray. Several miles outside of town, we passed what seemed to be a prison camp. The watchtowers and barbed-wire fence were grim and forbidding.

By now there was no doubt in our minds as to our destination. It was Siberia, for sure. Yes, but where in Siberia? Orientation was not one of our virtues, and with no map it was a lot of guesswork. To my mother it made no difference where in particular we were going: as far as she was concerned, all of Siberia was bad.

The train picked up speed, as if hastening to arrive at our destination before winter set in.

I woke up one morning and there it was—Novosibirsk: "New Siberia." The Siberia of my childish imagination was very cold, with blowing winds and snow drifts piled up to the rooftops. Outside, the morning was indeed chilly and overcast. Yet there was no snow.

The guards ordered us to prepare for disinfection and bathing. As we did so, another trainload of refugees arrived. We were not allowed to visit them, so we talked to them by shouting from a distance. Soon the guards chased us away. Still, we had been able to learn that their lot was worse than ours. They were kept locked up for the entire trip, and were treated as common prisoners.

At noontime we were told to take our possessions and follow a guard to the disinfecting tank. There we were ordered to leave our clothing in bundles with our nametags on them, to be deloused, and to proceed naked to the nearby Turkish baths. The bathhouse was a large facility, and was packed with people. We were allowed to enter in shifts to clean up. Papa, Moshe, and I settled down in a corner to scrub ourselves down. The thick steam, emanating from heated rocks sprinkled with water, caused us to perspire profusely. There was no soap, so each of us took turns slapping the back of his neighbor with brooms made of willow branches to loosen the dirt. After we did so, my father poured a bucket of water to rinse us off. We continued this for a while, and when finished our skin was as red as beets. I believe that we shed our top layers of skin along with the dirt. We had no towels, so we let the air dry our bodies and proceeded to pick up our clothing.

Our clothes were hot to the touch, and some of them were scorched from being "cooked" in the high-temperature disinfection tank. The clothing had not been washed, but it was rid of the crawling things that had infested it for so many weeks. It felt good to wear our clothes, at least for a while, without having to scratch ourselves all the time.

When we returned to our boxcar, we found that it, too, had been cleaned. Some sort of anitseptic smell lingered inside. Everybody reclaimed their positions in the car and bedded down for the night. You never really sleep well, however, on a hardboard bunk in a crowded freight-car. You sort of cat-nap. The rat-a-tat-tat clatter of the wheels over the steel rails, the locomotive's whistle blowing, the snoring and crying at night, the nightmare screams of your neighbor—all of it makes for a restless night.

I woke up in the morning to the smell of pines. We had left Novosibirsk and were traveling through the seemingly endless Siberian forest called taiga. The train stopped in a small town, itself called Taiga, where we were given some food. Papa went into town to try his luck at finding more food, but came back empty handed. All there was to be found for sale was *makhorka*, a low-grade Russian tobacco. Two hours later we moved on, the taiga walling us in on both sides.

We passed Tomsk without stopping. All I can recall from Tomsk are the red propaganda banners at the rail station. How much longer, I wondered, would we have to endure this cursed train? How big is Siberia? Where were they taking us? These questions were on everyone's mind.

We got our answer about one day's travel beyond Tomsk when we came to a little place called Asino. Here the rail tracks came to a dead end, with the eternal taiga all around. It had been nearly four weeks since we boarded the train in Lubomel, and we were enormously relieved to get off. Now a new feeling of suspense took over. What could we expect next?

In Asino we found much company like ourselves. Thousands of refugees inhabited the place, living in makeshift booths fashioned out of branches from the nearby trees. We nicknamed the booths "Sukkoth," after the holiday which commemorates the protection of the children of Israel during the Exodus from Egypt. Our family set out to the forest to gather up branches, and before long we had constructed our own "sukka."

The administrative headquarters responsible for the distribution of the refugees was set up in a nearby camp where the NKVD had an office and several barracks for the sick. The sick were tended by a *vratch* or medic, who made the rounds and told everyone *budyet khorosho*, "you will be well." But because that was all the medicine he had to dispense, the serious cases usually died.

On a chilly morning three days later we were told to get ready to ship out. Several trucks, each laden with refugees, took us a few miles into the forest over a bumpy road made up completely of logs. Eventually we arrived at yet another transition camp, this one nestled on the banks of the Chulym, a tributary of the river Ob. It was the widest river I had ever seen. The murky water was flowing north, making its way eventually to the Arctic Ocean. Moored to the river bank were several barges being loaded with refugees. We settled down to wait our turn to board a barge.

One thing we now knew for certain: it would be nearly impossible to escape from wherever it was they were taking us.

Meanwhile the mosquitoes descended on us like a dark cloud. No matter how much I slapped and chased them away, they seemed to be able to pierce my skin and fill themselves with my blood. Some of the mosquitoes were nearly one inch long. We built a large bonfire hoping that the smoke would chase away the pests.

In the late afternoon our group began to board a barge. To keep the barge in balance, the captain divided us into equal groups and advised us not to move around the deck. The barge was flat, and about thirty feet wide by eighty feet long. We were told that it was normally used to transport logs. It was getting dark and cold, so Moshe and I curled up on top of our belongings and soon fell asleep.

I was awakened in the gray morning by a slight rocking motion and the chug-chug of a motor. The barge, now roped to a tugboat, was being pulled slowly upstream.

We stopped once to take on provisions of bread and salted pike packed in barrels. The fish and bread tasted good, but made everyone very thirsty. To quench our thirst we drank river water.

For us children the barge trip was an adventure, but the adults were very worried. They speculated about the prospect of getting back to civilization, and about what they would be required to do in this desolate place. All around us was the taiga. It seemed as if the river, by means of its own sheer might, was carving a path through the dense forest.

Finally the barge captain informed us that we did not have much farther to go. Before long I saw lights flickering in the distance. As we came nearer, I realized that the lights were bonfires made by refugees who had preceded us.

Here, too, the refugees had built booths out of tree branches. They kept fires going to ward off the giant Siberian mosquitoes.

The barge docked alongside the riverbank and we disembarked at this nameless camp. Some time after we had left the train, our guards disappeared and were replaced by other men. These new masters told us to settle down and await transportation.

We found an abandoned booth, to which we added more branches so as to keep the mosquitoes out. We moved in and prepared to wait some more.

We lived in that booth for three days. On the third day horse-drawn wagons came to transport us to yet another location, from which we were to be dispatched to our final destination. Our family was the last one to leave. We loaded up a little wagon, which was drawn by one small horse and driven by a native Siberian of Tartar stock. We attempted to converse with the driver, but he would not speak to us. The only talking he did was when the horse slowed down, and then he let loose a chain of curses. The horse seemed to understand, because he always responded by speeding up.

The wagon took us on a dirt road full of mud-holes into the taiga. We constantly had to make our way around fallen tree-trunks. The deep mud-holes were laid over with logs to make the road passable. Every time the wagon had to be pulled out of a hole or over a large log, the poor horse had to strain very hard. Sometimes we helped push the wagon, for fear that the horse might collapse and we would be stranded in the middle of the forest. The thick trees pressed in upon us like two dark walls. In many places the road was so overgrown with foliage that we had to hold back the branches to keep from getting hit by them. Swarms of mosquitoes kept landing on us, and by the time we could feel their bite, they had already drawn blood. Our faces and hands were stained red with their splattered remains. They even bit us through our clothing.

Every so often we passed a clearing where potatoes were being grown or where there was evidence of logging.

After about three hours, we saw the lights of bonfires flickering amongst the trees. Night had fallen and it was getting chilly when we finally reached the *zavod*.

I never understood why the place was called *zavod*, for there was no factory there—just log cabins and barracks. The only thing even close to a factory was a metal workshop.

The driver dropped us off next to one of the bonfires and left. There was no one there to check us in or give us instructions about where to go or what to do. My parents picked a spot next to one of the bonfires, joining a group of hollow-eyed people staring into space. What were their thoughts? What would the future bring? How long were we going to be here? None of us had the answers to these questions. All the while, the mosquitoes continued to bite us.

I tried to get some sleep on the floor of one of the barracks, but to no avail. After dozing off briefly, I was awakened by things crawling over my face. I jumped up and was shocked to discover huge bedbugs all over me. I ran outside brushing and shaking my clothes to get rid of the insects. Some of those bedbugs were as big as a good-sized button. When I squashed them, blood—probably my own—oozed out, and they smelled like stinkbugs. The places on my body where I had been bitten swelled up. There was a red puncture-mark in the center of each welt, and they itched just like mosquito bites.

I spent the rest of the night sitting near the bonfire.

When morning finally arrived, I took a look around. The *zavod* was actually the administrative camp for the area. There was a medical dispensary, a kitchen with a dining area (consisting of benches and picnic-tables made of splintered pine), four long barracks for housing workers, four outhouses joined together, one water-well, one Turkish-style bath house, and a log cabin for the commandant and some guards. The bath had no running water, so water had to be brought from the nearby well in buckets. The steam oven consisted of huge boulders heated by burning wood. When water was splashed onto the hot rocks, it turned into steam and filled the inside of the bathhouse. The steam kept the bathhouse hot and humid, enabling a person to wash or scrub with a bath-broom, since we had no soap.

(Some months later, Papa and Moshe and I were scrubbing down at the bathhouse and enjoying the hot steam when the doors burst open and a group of nude Russian women poured in laughing and talking. With total disregard for our presence, they proceeded to wash themselves. Papa turned us around so we were facing the wall, hurriedly dried us off, and whisked us away.)

Later that morning, we received coupons for soup to be served in the dining hall. One coupon per person, and you were entitled to one portion of a watery cabbage soup, no refills. After this thin breakfast, we were assembled by local officials who divided us into three groups so that we could be sent to our permanent housing.

Mechanics, metal workers, machinists and clerks were to remain in the *zavod*. That left the other two groups. One group was to go to a village called Semyonovka, about five kilometers away. The other was destined for a place named Sukhoy-Log—the village of "Dry Gulch," to which our family was assigned.

A horse-drawn wagon carried our belongings, and we followed the wagon to our new home in Sukhoy-Log. The dirt road wound between tree stumps and small brush. After a brief journey the settlement emerged from the taiga. The entire village was composed of two long streets with log cabins on either side. In the middle of each street was a water-well with a wooden bucket attached to a long pole with a counterweight on the other end. Each cabin came with a plot of land of about one acre for growing vegetables. In the center of the village was a school, along with the standard Red Corner with its supply of propaganda magazines. Next to it was a small store where one could obtain rationed supplies when they were available.

About half of the log cabins were hollow shells, with no doors, windows, or floors. The rest of the cabins were occupied by Russians, Ukrainians, and Tartars. Some of these were, like us, "Special Resettlers," while others had been exiled for "anti-communist activities" and elected to remain there when they had served out their sentences. There was also a number of free-settlers, including teachers, administrators, and loggers.

The driver dropped us off at one of the log cabin duplexes. One half of the cabin was occupied by a worn-out Russian woman with two teenaged daughters. The other half of the duplex was empty, having evidently been stripped of anything that could be carried away. My family naturally assumed that this half was reserved for us, and began to move in. But when the official in charge of housing came by, he ordered us to stop at once and move in with the Russian woman and her daughters. The poor woman protested, and so did we. But the official was insistent. He said the room would be refitted shortly, and that we could move in then, but not before. Reluctantly, we moved in with the Russian woman and assured her that we would stay out of her way. We settled down in the front corner of her ten-by-fifteen foot room, on the rough board floor.

It was early August of 1940. After the boxcar and the branch sheds, we finally had a roof over our heads. It was not an ideal situation, but it was better than what we had experienced in the previous two months. The *khozyaika*, as we called her—the "landlady"—was hostile at first, but in time became more friendly. I think she appreciated having company. At any rate, she helped to prepare us for the coming winter by telling us how to collect wood for heating and how to deal with the cold.

The *khozyaika* had very few possessions: a rough wooden table, two benches next to the window, a few pots and pans hanging from the wall, some old photos, a Russian oven, and some blankets. All the clothes she and her girls owned were on their backs. The wood-burning oven took up about a fifth of the cabin. It resembled a baker's oven, with a flat top which served as a bed. It was actually a clever design. The rising heat served to keep one warm during the long winter nights.

The floor of the cabin was made of splintered pine boards. Under the floor was a deep hole in the ground, accessible by means of a trap door, that served as a root cellar for storing and preserving potatoes and other vegetables for winter use.

The woman and her two daughters sustained themselves by farming some of the land carved out of the taiga, picking berries and pine cones, and tapping birch trees for sweet syrup. Our Russian and Tartar neighbors on either side also had some chickens and a cow. They were somewhat better off than our *khozyaika*, because they had men in their families to help with the farming. Our *khozyaika*, however, seemed to be old and frail.

The woman told us the following story about her family:

"We were sent to this place by the government twelve years ago, in 1928. Before that, we were well-to-do farmers, and owned much land. But when Stalin took over, we were labeled *kulaks*. All of our land and possessions were confiscated. My husband was accused of being a counter-revolutionary, and we were sent into exile. When we arrived here in Siberia, we had to cut down the trees and build our own log cabins. The hardship, disease, and hunger killed my husband. The same fate awaits you. No one leaves Siberia."

My parents were already depressed, and the woman's story did little to cheer us. Mama began to cry, and the woman joined her. But Papa became upset and scolded both of them. "We are not Soviet citizens," he told the *khozyaika*. "We are not going to be here forever like you."

We bedded down on the floor for the first night's sleep. The *khozyaika* and her two daughters climbed up on the oven. The burning embers in the oven spread a nice warmth throughout the cabin, and soon I was asleep. But it was not long before I was awakened by something dripping on me. It was raining, and the roof was leaking. I repositioned myself in another spot, only to be awakened once again by bedbugs. Yes, they were here, too—coming out of the crevices in the logs where they lived. Worn out, tired, and hungry as I was, however, I finally fell asleep, in spite of the dripping ceiling and the vermin.

In the morning, a messenger came to the village to inform us of a meeting to be held at the *zavod* in front of the commandant's office. "All 'Special Resettlers,'" we were told, "must attend the meeting, which is to be held right after the distribution of the breakfast soup." The office of *Tovarishch* (Comrade) Krestov, the area commandant, was just a few yards from the kitchen. After we finished drinking our portions of soup, Moshe and I joined the crowd in front of the commandant's office. Several minutes later, Tovarishch Krestov came out wearing his uniform and sidearm. He was accompanied by several armed guards. Krestov stopped on the steps leading up to his office, so that he could look down over the assembly. He scanned the people in silence, and then with a slow and deliberate voice he began:

"*Spyets-Pereselentsy*, we brought you here to work in the taiga, which you can see all around you. You will develop this area and build lodgings for yourselves and your families. Do not try to escape or leave. It will be futile to do so. No one has ever succeeded in doing so. Any one caught trying to escape will be arrested and shot."

"We hope that you will develop this area into a big city. Each one of you will receive some farming land and a cow. It will take a while, but you will get used to living here. Those who do not learn to live here will perish. It is therefore to your advantage to learn fast and adjust quickly."

"All males ages sixteen to sixty will be obliged to work. Anyone under sixteen years old will have to go to school, and will receive a free education in order to become a productive citizen of the U.S.S.R. If you are late to work without a permit from the doctor, 25% of your pay will be deducted. Being late twice will cause you to lose 50% of your pay. Three times, and you will be sentenced to three months in jail."

"Every working person will receive four hundred grams of bread per day, plus some provisions from the supply store. Agitation, propaganda, and black market speculation are unlawful. Violators will be punished by law with a term of five to ten years in prison. Revolts and instigations of revolts are punishable by the firing squad."

"Are there any questions?"

One of the men in the assembly, a baker by trade, asked if it was legal to impose such restrictions on us since we were not Soviet citizens. Tovarishch Krestov did not reply, but gave him a stern look. Then we were ordered to disperse. The next morning we heard that the baker was arrested during the night and taken away.

Our village was divided into sectors. Each sector was made up of several log cabins, with an average of eight to ten people per cabin. One man was designated by the commandant's office to be in charge in each sector for the purpose of reporting and relaying messages. Ration cards were distributed for each dependent. The rations were to be received twice monthly, at least in theory. The problem was that the supply house usually did not receive supplies; furthermore, when supplies did come in, there were never enough to go around. It was rumored that the supplies had been stolen before they reached the supply house. In the meantime, we were being served soup in the *zavod* kitchen, until things "normalized."

Plans were set in motion to rebuild the abandoned log cabins, and we were excited at the prospect of having our own place to live. A large pit was dug at the edge of the forest for the purpose of firing clay bricks. The bricks were to be used for building cooking and heating ovens in the log cabins that were being repaired. All of us pitched in and repaired the floors and windows. We built and installed doors, cleaned out the cellars, and stuffed moss mixed with mud into the cracks of the cabin walls and the spaces between the logs. Everyone pitched in to beat the approaching Siberian winter.

Moshe and I helped Papa build a bed for the family to sleep in. The bed was about king-size, made of rough pine boards splintered from a tree by using an axe and a series of wedges. It was actually a square box about six inches deep with four legs attached to it. We gathered up some moss, dry straw, and hay to fill the bed, and covered it all with a blanket. All four of us slept in that bed, with Moshe and I lying crosswise at our parents' feet. The walls of our cabin received a good coat of whitewash to make them look bright and clean. Bricklayers built a brick oven for us. The oven was about four feet by three feet, with two burner-openings for cooking. The chimney extended all the way to the ceiling, so that its entire height generated heat when the oven was fired up.

We were ready to move into our new living quarters. Our *khozyaika* was glad to get rid of us, and vice-versa, but we remained good neighbors.

Due to a shortage of refurbished cabins, ten people had to be assigned to each one. Wolf and Frieda moved in with us, plus another family of four (including a one-year-old baby and a seven-year-old boy). Each family occupied a corner of the cabin. The fourth corner was taken up by the brick oven. There were ten souls in an area of about two hundred twenty-five square feet.

Each family lived around its bed. Papa and Wolf built a table and two benches, which they used as a dividing line between us and the other family. There was no outhouse. Personal needs were taken care of in the forest behind some trees. Laundry was also done outdoors. Since there was no soap, Mama boiled our clothes in a big pot to kill any vermin, and then hung them out to dry. Our underwear and shirts were clean, although they still looked dirty.

All adult males were given jobs. Papa, Wolf, and some of the other men were assigned to cutting down trees and preparing them for transportation. The logging was done manually, with long handsaws and axes. The loggers tied the felled trees with chains and used workhorses to drag them to the nearby river. Once there, the logs were floated to the mill.

Logging, of course, is dangerous work. None of the refugees had done it before, and several of them were eventually killed by falling timber.

In Siberia we were called by new Russian names. Moshe was Meesha, I was called Ezya, my father Wolf became Volodya, and my mother Shayndl became Zhenya. Along with our new names, we gradually acquired a sense of how to live.

The kitchen at the *zavod* was supposed to supply soup to the workers and their families at a fixed price until everyone settled down and became self-sufficient. When my mother had no provisions, she would give Moshe and me what little money she had so that we could buy soup from the kitchen. She once gave us one ruble, with which we were to split a portion of soup. We were both very hungry. As we walked to the *zavod*, I kept trying to figure out how to get more to eat. I knew very well that one portion (about a liter) was not going to satisfy our hunger pangs. But I could not think of any way to stretch our money.

At the kitchen, we walked over to the cashier and handed over our ruble. The cashier took his pencil and wrote out a coupon: "1 soup—1 ruble." He handed the coupon back to me without looking up. As I took the coupon, it struck me: why not rewrite it? I could simply replace "1 soup" with "2 soups" and "1 ruble" with "2 rubles."

I told Moshe to wait a couple of minutes while I went into one of the out-houses. Once inside, I locked the door and very meticulously proceeded to erase and rewrite the coupon. After that, I took my place in line to get the soup. My heart was pounding and my knees were shaking for fear of being caught. At the kitchen window I handed the coupon and the soup-pan to the cook. Without looking up, the cook poured in two portions of the watery soup, and even added a little extra! Moshe was sitting at a table waiting for me. His eyes widened when he saw how much soup I had, so I told him what I had done. We both drank the soup quickly and ran out of the dining hall.

Uncle Wolf happened to be nearby, so I approached him with a proposition: If he bought a coupon for one ruble, I would get him four soups. He laughed and said "How are you going to do that?" When I told him, he quit smirking. It was a clever idea, he said, but not proper. But as he was hungry, he was willing to give it a try.

Wolf purchased a coupon, and I changed the 1 to a 4. This time I was a bit more confident. Again the cook did not look up, and poured four portions of soup into my container. Wolf, Frieda, Moshe and I split the soup between us.

My gimmick of stealing soup gradually grew more bold. Rather than erase the numbers, I simply changed them from a 1 to a 7 for Wolf and Frieda and from a 1 to a 10 (by simply adding a 0) for my own family. Moshe and I used a bucket and a stick to carry the soup home, which was about a mile away. Mama told us that it was not right to steal, but in this case it was justified because of our gnawing hunger; besides, she said, "the cook steals the provisions and just adds water to the pot." She soon learned to add a few things to the soup to make it taste better.

My parents were worried every time Moshe and I went to the *zavod* to get soup, but our hunger far outstripped our money. I even changed several coupons for the other family in our cabin.

One time I was standing in line at the kitchen waiting to get ten portions of soup when Tovarishch Krestov walked in. When he saw me with my bucket, he came over and asked "Who is this bucket for?" I hesitated for a moment and then replied, "Oh, it is for the Stakhanovite group of lumberjacks, Commandant." (Stakhanov was a miner who produced far more than his output quota, and Stakhanovites were workers honored for their exceptional diligence.) "Well that is my most efficient brigade," he replied. "Come on, sonny, the Stakhanovites get first preference"—and he walked me right up to the front of the line.

I was scared to death. When we left the kitchen Moshe and I ran all the way home, while being careful not to spill any of the soup. I did not want to go back to the kitchen for soup ever again. But hunger prevailed, and I did return.

My soup-stealing venture lasted nearly three weeks. But all thieves eventually get caught.

Apparently the kitchen management suspected something was up, because they changed the format of the coupons. I studied the new coupons and believed that I could alter them successfully. But I could not figure out the codified numbers that they had added, and these ultimately gave me away.

After I had presented a forged coupon at the kitchen window, the head cook came out and grabbed my arm. He pulled me into the kitchen and said that he would keep me there until my parents came to get me. Seeing this, Moshe ran home and came back with Mama. She stormed into the kitchen, demanding to know why they were treating her boy like a criminal. "He *is* a criminal," the head cook replied, "he was stealing soup." "He is just a hungry boy," my mother pleaded. The cook replied that if she would give him two hundred rubles, he would agree to forget the whole thing. "You could just as well ask for two thousand rubles," she said, "because I don't have the money." "And," she added, "if you go to the commandant I will tell him that you steal provisions and replace them with water, and also that you tried to blackmail me." The argument continued until Mama finally took me by the arm and marched me out of the kitchen.

That ended the soup episode. I never went to the kitchen again, and in any case the program of selling soup to the refugees was soon abolished.

My thirteenth birthday fell on August 20, 1940. Jewish tradition holds that thirteen is the age at which a boy becomes a man. In recognition of this fact, my mother took me to see a man who lived in a crowded barracks with perhaps a hundred other people. This fellow, who had a beard and was supposedly a rabbi, taught me a prayer or two as well as the art of putting on *tfillin* (phylacteries) such as my father used to wear in the synagogue. I was glad to know how to put on *tfillin*, even though I did not own any. But that one visit was the only time I ever went to see the rabbi, and in fact the only time I ever practiced religion in the Soviet Union—for in the U.S.S.R. it was unlawful to teach religion or conduct any religious activities.

When I looked back many years later on my visit to the rabbi, I realized that this humble ceremony was my Bar Mitzvah.

As autumn approached, the taiga was overflowing with all sorts of wild berries and the huge pine cones contained ripe nuts for the picking. I was afraid to venture deep into the forest for fear of getting lost, so I asked our neighbor's daughters if they would take us along with them when they went.

Olga, who was fourteen or fifteen, claimed to know her way in the forest. So one bright and warm day, Moshe and I and the other boy from our cabin followed Olga and her younger sister into the forest.

Deep in the taiga we found lots of berries and pine cones. As we followed Olga's lead, the forest became more dense and the mosquitoes more vicious. My hands were stained from the berries and so was my face from slapping the mosquitoes. Soon our bags were full and we were ready to return home. I asked Olga if she could find her way back because I could not. Olga looked around uncertainly. I climbed a tall pine tree to get a better view, but all I could see were more trees. We shouted, and were greeted only by the echo of our own voices. Olga suggested that we walk west with the setting sun. We did so until we finally came to a trail, and then continued on the trail until a village came into view. It was Semyonovka, about five miles away from our village of Sukhoy-Log. From there we walked home on the dirt road.

Mama was in tears when we arrived. She said that they were ready to form a search party to find us. The berries and pine nuts, however, were a treat for everybody. From then on, I stayed within sight of the village when I ventured into the forest.

One day, the commandant's office issued a bulletin asking for volunteers to be transferred to the city of Asbest. My mother was successful in getting our family registered to go. "Anywhere has to be better than Siberia" was my parent's motto. Unfortunately, Frieda and Wolf did not manage to get on the list. Mama tried to persuade the registration clerk to add my aunt and uncle to the list, but he refused on the ground that the quota had been filled. Mama was not one to give up easily, and kept begging the clerk to add my aunt and uncle. But the clerk became irritated. "Very well," he said, "since you want to be with your relatives so much, I will take you off the list and add someone else." This was not what my mother had in mind, but her pleas fell on deaf ears. Needless to say, my parents were very disappointed and upset. As it turned out it was probably for the best, because the conditions in Asbest, as I've said, were probably worse than in Siberia.

Yet life in Siberia was very hard. Our little cabin was seriously overcrowded, and we were always hungry. The rationed food supplies were insufficient, and in any case the work in the forest did not pay enough money to make up the difference. There were not enough doctors to treat the sick, and even if there had been, there was no medicine available at any cost. Many people became ill from malaria and malnutrition. These people often died, especially the elderly and the very young.

The discontent and desperation among the refugees finally led to a showdown. The refugees decided to stage a mass exodus—something that was unheard of under the Soviet regime, and was punishable by imprisonment or death.

The organizers of this exodus decided that we would build carts on wheels made from cross-sections of large pine trees. The carts were supposed to hold our belongings as well as those people who were unable to walk. The plan was for the refugees in Semyonovka to start the march towards Sukhoy-Log. Then we were to join them, and together we would walk to the river and force the authorities to supply barges to take us to the nearest train station.

Papa and Wolf built a cart, and we prepared to join the Semyonovka refugees when they arrived. But Commandant Krestov got word of our plans and met the Semyonovka group with armed guards on horseback. Some shots were fired, and the group's leaders were arrested and taken away. After that, the rest of the refugees dispersed and went back to their cabins.

Meanwhile, the people in our village were packed and ready with their pull-carts. We were waiting for the Semyonovka group to arrive when we were approached by the work-brigade leader, a tough Russian woman. "I wondered why you did not show up for work!" she exclaimed. "You fools! Just what do you think you will accomplish with this sort of behavior? You cannot get far. Compared to the power of the Soviet Socialist Republic, you are like a drop in the ocean! Go back to your homes before it is too late!"

How right she was. Ours was an act of futile desperation. We could never have made it out on our own. And just about then we found out what had happened in Semyonovka.

Beaten and demoralized, the *Spyets-Pereselentsy* returned to their cramped quarters to prepare for the Siberian winter. Maybe the old Russian *khozyaika* next door knew what she was saying when she told us that no one ever left Siberia.

The summer was coming to an end. The days were getting shorter and the nights longer. It was time for Moshe and me to go back to school. I enrolled in the sixth grade to continue from where I had left off five months earlier in the city of Guysin in the Ukraine. Moshe enrolled in the fourth grade.

The school building was a one-story complex constructed of logs. It went up to the seventh grade. The floor was made of rough boards and the desks were made of the same rough pine as the floor. The building had no electricity, but the windows were large enough to permit ample light to filter into the classroom. Each classroom was equipped with a wood-burning stove, but the stoves were for some reason never fired up. We used to freeze in those classrooms! The school was closed only when the temperature fell to negative fifty degrees centigrade, so during the winter we had to wear our overcoats and stomp our feet to keep warm.

I began school full of enthusiasm for the new subjects of algebra, Russian grammar and literature, world geography, Roman history, and German language. About thirty students enrolled in my class, but two-thirds of them were generally absent due to sickness, lack of warm clothing, or lack of interest. The school authorities did not seem to bother with absenteeism. There were times when only five children were in attendance in my class.

My favorite subjects were Russian literature and Roman history. We had no books to study from and there was no library either. All classes were conducted by the teachers in the form of lectures, and sometimes the teacher just read from a book. We had no notepads or writing paper. In order to take notes in class I used to write on leftover newspapers that we took from the Red Corner. I had to scribble in large script, for otherwise the ink ran together with the print on the newspapers and it became impossible to decipher my notes. To emphasize important ideas I printed in bold letters. I had stacks upon stacks of these newspapers with notes.

A student was allowed to borrow the teacher's book for two evenings to copy the lecture or memorize it. I recall memorizing one section of the Russian grammar book for three whole months. As a reward for attaining a grade of "5," the top grade in any given course, students were promised a new book on the subject. I attained a "5" in Roman history, and was told that a book had been ordered and would be awarded to me as soon as it arrived. I was looking forward to receiving my prize book, but it never came.

The same man who taught Roman history also taught German. He was a hunchback, but a wonderful teacher as well as a wonderful person. His ability to hold the class's attention was extraordinary, and he took as much time as needed to be sure that everyone understood the subject. He seemed to have a special love for Roman history, and his accounts of various Roman wars and battles were spiced with such rich details that they kept me spellbound.

As for German, it was easy for me. It sounded like Yiddish, and practically all I had to do was speak Yiddish when reciting my words. I earned a "5" in German as well. One of my classmates was a Jewish girl from Germany, and she was given an honorary "5" and excused from attending the class altogether.

Algebra was a tough subject for me. I memorized the rules and formulas but did not understand them. I had attended only four months of the fifth grade in the Ukraine, and hadn't learned enough math in preparation for algebra. My teacher also moved very fast, and not having books for reference or study compounded the difficulty.

My friend Popov, a classmate, was good at algebra. Popov's mother was a schoolteacher, so I used to go over to his home to do my homework. In the end I passed algebra largely because I had memorized most of the formulas, but I did not comprehend much of it until many years later.

The educational system in the Soviet Union portrayed capitalism as evil and exploitative, and emphasized the struggle of the proletariat. In Roman history, for instance, Spartacus was portrayed as a great hero. According to the Soviets, Spartacus was the first proletarian leader, and he set an example by trying to free his fellow slaves from oppression. Another example is a poem we had to learn that told of "Mister Twister the ex-Minister, the dealer and banker, the owner of factories, newspapers, and steamships," who decided for his pleasure to tour around the world. The poem went on to proclaim that Mister Twister's lifestyle was made possible only through the labor of his exploited workers.

Geography class was conducted with the aid of a huge map on the blackboard. We had no atlases, so we had to memorize the various features of the map, including rivers, mountains, borders, and so forth. Here again, the teacher told us that the red star of the U.S.S.R. had five points because it represented the five continents of the world that were eventually to be conquered by the proletariat. The teachers also emphasized the many British colonies by highlighting them in green on the map. "England," he said, "is using their guns to enslave the people of the world and is stealing their natural resources to benefit the English capitalists."

To do any homework in our cabin was nearly impossible because of the noise, inadequate lighting, and lack of space. I used to go to the Red Corner or to Popov's house to study. On many occasions I was rewarded by an invitation from Mrs. Popov to stay for dinner.

I also made friends with my neighbor two houses down—Volodya Shtshedrin, a seventeen year-old native Siberian. Volodya and I talked a lot about the places I had been to. He was interested in the world outside Sukhoy-Log, the only place he had ever known. Soon after, Volodya was drafted into the Red Army, and I never saw him again.

A couple of my classmates were Poles, but I could not take the initiative to befriend them. My memories of Poland would not allow me to do so. I felt much more comfortable with the Soviet boys and girls. I also became friends with the German-Jewish girl I spoke of earlier, but she was sick most of the time so I did not see her very often.

October came, and with it came snow, frost, howling winds, and snow drifts sometimes seven to ten feet high. One morning I woke up to find the front of our cabin covered by a great drift. The men of the house struggled to push the door open so that we could slip through to dig ourselves out.

The government supply-house issued all outdoor workers special clothing —padded cotton pants and jackets, heavy padded hats with earmuffs, gloves, and thick, knee-high felt boots. No socks were available, so the men wrapped their feet in newspapers or rags. The rest of us non-workers had to rely on our own ingenuity to protect ourselves from the harsh cold weather.

To get around in the snow, the natives used skis made from split pine planks. The boards were cut to size, and one side was whittled smooth with a sharp ax. The skis were then tied in three places with the smooth sides facing each other. To shape the skis, one inserted bricks or wooden blocks in between them near the front, middle, and end, and then dried the rig next to an oven for several days. The final task was to nail on a shoe-sized platform with a leather strap or rope, and the skis were then ready for use. Every so often they had to be reshaped and dried, but they served the purpose. On mornings when the snow was fresh and deep, I used a set of skis to make my way to school. Popov and I also had much fun skiing down the hill near the edge of the village.

The Siberian winter was in full fury as we entered the year 1941. Not only was the winter our enemy, but so was starvation. The government-supplied food provisions often simply "disappeared" before reaching their destination. The NKVD cracked down by applying death sentences to anyone caught stealing food supplies, but even death threats did not deter some people from stealing. And there were rumors that the NKVD itself was involved in stealing food.

Moshe and I sometimes went out to fields that had already been harvested in order to search for overlooked potatoes under the snow. The few potatoes we found were usually frozen and tasted terrible, but we ate them anyway. When the food rations did come through, we had to stand in line to buy whatever it was they were selling. It was always wise to be among the first in line, because in most cases the supply store ran out about two-thirds of the way down the line. Once, when word was out that supplies had arrived, I put on my father's winter clothes in addition to my own and went out at 1:00 AM to stand in line. At such times it was not unusual for the temperature to be negative fifty degrees centigrade or even colder. Even this early in the morning, I was third or fourth in line. About four hours later Mama came out to replace me so I could go home and return my father's winter clothes, without which he could not go to work.

In Siberia, the winter weather can change without warning into a blizzard with howling winds and flying snow or ice. On such days visibility is near zero. When caught in such weather you must stay on the compacted trail to find your way home. If you veer off the trail it is easy to lose your sense of direction, get lost, and possibly freeze to death.

Moshe and I were in school one day when the temperature suddenly dropped and the wind began to shriek and howl. School let out and everyone was told to go home at once. I ran over to Moshe's classroom and we left school in single file, walking along the trail to our house at the end of the village. The blowing snow felt like tiny missiles hitting our faces and stinging our eyes. We had trouble walking without losing our balance, and we had to lean forward to overcome the force of the wind. When I finally reached our cabin, the first words Mama said to me were "Where is your brother?" "Behind me," I replied. But Moshe was not behind me. Mama, Wolf, and I ran out and retraced my steps. About a hundred yards from the cabin I saw Moshe. He was a few feet off the trail, waist deep in the snow, and facing in the wrong direction. We pulled him up and took him home. In the cabin we discovered that his nose and ears had turned white and were nearly frostbitten. Mama began to warm him up by rubbing snow on his ears and nose and then using warm water to stimulate his circulation. Moshe said that he had been calling for me, but I had heard nothing but the howling wind. It was a horrifying experience. Had Moshe strayed any further from the trail, we might not have found him in time to save him from frostbite or even death.

At one point that winter, all the refugees in our area who were working as lumberjacks—including of course my father—were ordered to report to Tsudbargy, a village about thirty kilometers away. Several weeks later, my father returned home. When he walked into the cabin we could barely recognize him. He had grown a beard and lost much weight, and he smelled awful. In Tsudbargy, he told us, they were put to work with political prisoners under prison conditions. Some of the older prisoners had fought in the armies of the tsar, for which the communist revolutionaries had slapped them with long terms of penal servitude. They labored under the supervision of guards accompanied by dogs. Papa was supposed to receive better food than the prisoners, as well as wages of thirty rubles a month. None of it materialized. He was never paid and he received prisoner's fare—a watery soup called *shtchee*. One day, he simply walked away from his job and trekked the thirty kilometers to Sukhoy-Log. When he came home, Mama reported to the officials that he was sick—which was not far from the truth. As we discovered later, most of the "free" men followed in his footsteps.

For an outhouse during the winter we dug out a hole in the snow about five feet square, perhaps a hundred feet away from the cabin. To keep our clothes free from lice, Mama simply hung them outside for the night. This froze the insects. In the morning we had to thaw out our clothes, but all the crawling things were dead. Some of us nevertheless developed open sores, especially on the legs. These were not from insect bites, however, but from vitamin deficiencies.

In the end, we survived the winter. We tended to our illnesses and ate what we could find. Sometimes the non-edible became edible, and we learned to live with it. As Commandant Kristov said when we first arrived in Sukhoy-Log, we had to learn fast if we wanted to survive. It became clear to us how right he was when the winter finally came to an end in April of 1941. When we emerged from our cabins after nearly six months of virtual hibernation, we met people we had not seen since the fall. To our sorrow, some of our neighbors had died during the winter months from starvation, disease, depression, or all of these combined.

Around this time, Mama had an accident. While chopping wood for the stove, she missed the log and struck her foot. The blade of the ax cut through her shoe and sliced into her left foot between her first two toes. She was bleeding profusely, but our neighbor managed to stop the bleeding with bandages. Moshe and I carried her all the way to the clinic at the *zavod*. In the clinic a nurse poured a lot of iodine on the wound and re-bandaged her foot. We then carried her back to the cabin. Fortunately for her and for us, the foot did not become infected and healed properly.

In May we received a food parcel from my mother's sister Luba, who lived in the city of Penza about two hundred miles west of Kuybyshev in central Russia. It contained canned meat, vegetables, and some clothing. Mama had to walk about three miles to the Semyonovka post office to claim the package. A month later we received another food package from them. The parcels were a godsend, as they came at a time when we had no food at all.

With spring came the budding trees and flowers. The sap began to flow in the birch trees, and I learned to tap them to collect syrup. Popov and I also went out to the river to do some fishing. Unfortunately my homemade hook did not hold the fish. Popov was lucky to catch four little perch, which he carried home in his tea kettle. I was able to find some pine cones and extracted the nuts from them to take home, so at least I did not return empty-handed. I wish I had made a bow and some arrows to hunt for squirrels or rabbits. But the thought never entered my mind. Being a city boy, I knew nothing of such things.

To prepare for the next winter, we decided to grow some vegetables on the strip of land adjacent to our cabin. Mama claimed some expertise in farming. She was raised on a small farm and still remembered a thing or two. Everyone in our cabin pitched in turning the soil, weeding, and making rows for planting potatoes. The soil was rich with mulch from decaying trees and vegetation, and it was easy to work. Mama made a bed of straw mixed with cow manure and soil in preparation for planting carrots, cucumbers, and cabbage. The neighbors helped out by donating some leftover seed and potato peelings for planting potatoes. We planted the seed and potato peelings and let nature do the rest.

The locals had been farming for many years, but none of them had developed much land. They told us that it was not worth it: because of the extremely heavy taxation, each family developed just enough land to supply their needs. The Tartar family next door had a cow and some chickens. Mama asked them why they had only one cow. "It is not worth the effort," she was told. "If you have more than one cow, you have to give the government a certain amount of milk and beef in lieu of tax." Some of our neighbors, however, farmed secret plots inside the forest.

After school Moshe and I helped out on our little "farm" by weeding and enlarging the potato mounds to ensure that all the potatoes were covered with soil. The potato plants progressed nicely and looked healthy. The specially prepared vegetable bed also yielded a nice crop. At the same time, the distribution center began to receive food supplies more often. Even though the supplies were still rationed, we were able to secure some flour and cereal, and occasionally even some salted pike. At last it looked as if we were not going to die from starvation.

School came to an end in May of 1941. I worked hard to prepare for my sixth-grade final examinations. I received top marks in all subjects and was promoted to the seventh grade.

Summer vacation was wonderful. Popov and I did some fishing and swimming. Papa, Moshe, and I went to the forest to collect pine cones, from which we extracted pine nuts. I would climb up the pine tree and shake the branches, and the others would collect the fallen pine cones. I used some pine wood to whittle out a propeller, mounted the propeller on a stick, and nailed it on the top of our roof facing the wind. The propeller spun whenever the wind was blowing. I liked my invention, but no one else did. The vibrations and noise of the spinning prop reverberated throughout our cabin and kept everybody awake at night. So I was forced to take down the prop.

One early morning at the end of June, we were standing in line for food rations when someone said that the Germans had invaded Russia. This was confirmed a month later, when we read it in an old newspaper. The paper denounced the Germans as "traitors" for not honoring their non-aggression treaty with the U.S.S.R. The Soviets also called the Germans "barbarians" because of their atrocities against Soviet citizens. "With the leadership of Comrade Stalin and Marshal Voroshilov," the paper wrote, "the Red Army will crush the German snake under the Soviet boot and pursue the Germans to their own land for a final victory."

The Red Corner was a busy place now, as the Soviet propaganda machine was in full swing. Almost everyone came over to listen to the loudspeaker or read the news about the war. The magazines featured German firing squads shooting peasant women and children and burning their villages. For the moment, it was clear that we were lucky to have been displaced to this far corner of the world. Otherwise we would have been caught up in the invasion of Russia. As it was, we were deeply concerned for our relatives in Lubomel as well as our friends in Guysin.

There were rumors that the Polish government-in-exile was forming an army of Polish refugees to fight the Germans alongside the allied armies. We began to feel that we might soon be getting out of Siberia. But as always, we were warned that no one ever managed to leave Siberia. "You will live here, and you will die here," we were told.

In late August of 1941, however, Commandant Krestov's office issued a bulletin. It proclaimed that the *Spyets-Pereselentsy* were free to leave! We were also informed that a schedule of transportation by horse and wagon would soon be published. The wagons would take us to the River Chulym and from there to the nearest railroad station.

Those who had lived and suffered in Siberia for many years could not believe it. But we had never lost hope that we would someday manage to leave this harsh and inhospitable place.

It was my fourteenth birthday.

Chapter Five

Uzbekistan

The potato patch we had planted in the early spring was ready for harvest by late August. All three families in our cabin joined forces to dig up the potatoes. We had no shovels or forks, so we used our hands. The crop was excellent. Each plant produced five or six large potatoes, some of them ten inches long. The other vegetables, including a small crop of cabbages, radishes, and cucumbers, were also ripe and ready to harvest. We ate most of the vegetables, of which there weren't many, but stored our share of the potatoes in the cellar under the cabin so that they would be preserved until our departure. Unfortunately, some field rats found the potatoes and feasted on them, so we got a big cat and put him in the cellar to eat the rats. The cat kept the rats in check, but many times came away from fighting them with wounds on his nose and face.

In September we received word from the commandant's office that horse-drawn wagons would be available in a few days to drive us to the river Chulym. There we were to board a barge that would take us to the rail station at Asino. Thus we would go back to Asino the same way we had come.

The news about our imminent departure stirred up all ten people in our cabin. As we had no other nourishment and no idea how long the trip would last, we all began working to convert the potatoes into transportable food. We peeled them and cut them up into tiny pieces. We then formed them into *latkes* or pancakes to be dried in our neighbor's oven until they were crisp. This made them easy to carry and less likely to spoil quickly. For the use of her good Russian-style oven, we rewarded the *khozyaika* with our furniture and some leftover potatoes that we could not have carried anyway. Our old blankets once again became bundles, only this time they were filled with as many potato pancakes as they could hold. Each of us carried as much as possible.

We had no idea what our destination would be, but we hoped to avoid living in a cold climate. We bid goodbye to Sukhoy-Log with no real regrets, although I personally had mixed feelings about leaving. I was happy to leave behind the sickness, hunger, and other harsh conditions we experienced in Siberia, but I would also take with me fond memories of friends, fishing, school, and the wild taiga. I could not say the same for my parents or the other families. Many of them had lost loved ones in one way or another, and others took with them permanent mementos of hardship in the form of fingers and toes that had been scarred or mutilated by frostbite.

The staging area for the departure was the *zavod*. We got up before dawn and walked there through the forest, our backs loaded with baggage. We looked like a long line of busy ants as we made our way down the trail.

At the *zavod* we found chaos and turmoil. Everyone was eager to leave without delay. People were milling around the wagons, each family hoping to get a big one. At last we secured a driver with a one-horse wagon to take us to the river. When all was ready the driver urged the horse forward with his whip, and thus after fourteen months in Siberia we once again spread our wings for a journey into the unknown.

When we pulled out of the *zavod*, I thought I saw a trace of envy in the eyes of those we were leaving behind.

This time the bumpy, log-strewn trail was familiar to us. Our high spirits were not dampened even when the first light snow of the season began to fall.

It was mid-afternoon when we arrived at the river. The place was swarming with refugees like us. Our driver dropped us off in a clearing next to the riverbank. The falling snow and overcast weather prompted us to construct a makeshift shelter out of branches in which we could pass the night.

When we had come to Siberia from Lubomel, we spent only one day by the banks of the Chulym. This time, however, things didn't move nearly as fast as before. The overcast days and long, cold nights made our wait seem endless. It was getting progressively colder, and we all huddled together and kept the fires going to keep warm at night. The mornings greeted us with dark skies, cold fog, and wet dew. Every day we waited anxiously for the arrival of the barge, but it did not come.

We had been on the river bank for over a week and were beginning to fear that a serious winter storm would catch us unprepared. The potato pancakes were running low and my mother cut our rations. The nearby village sold out of food. I tried my luck at fishing, but my homemade hook could hold neither bait nor fish.

Then one bright day a biplane landed on the grassy field near our camp. The pilot, who was in uniform, came over to survey the situation. He left after promising to get a barge to take us to Asino.

Moshe and I and some other kids ran over to the plane when it landed. To fly an airplane had always been my dream. My first real toy, made for me by my father, was a biplane with wheels fashioned from empty thread spools and a hand-carved propeller that turned when I blew on it. I had never seen a plane on the ground. The ones in the air looked tiny, and even though this was a single-seat biplane it seemed huge by comparison. I could not contain my excitement and had to touch the propeller and the smooth fabric of the fuselage. I wanted to climb into the cockpit but was chased away by the pilot.

When the plane took off, I watched until it disappeared over the tree line.

A couple of days later a huge barge pulled by a tugboat arrived at our camp. The barge lined up alongside the dock, several planks were lowered onto it, and we were ordered to board. To keep the vessel on an even keel, the captain had the passengers spread out over the deck and forbade us to walk around. There were probably several hundred of us on that barge.

When the tugboat engine roared, the steel cable tensed and the barge began to move down stream. Soon the captain opened a barrel of salted pike and passed out slices of black Russian bread and fish. It was delicious. I could easily have eaten three or four more portions, but had to be satisfied with my share.

Several hours later we arrived at another dock and disembarked. When we left the barge it was dark and snowing. We lit some fires and made camp by the dock for an overnight stay. Moshe and I fell asleep on our bundles, hugging each other to keep warm.

In the morning Papa and Wolf hired a wagon to take us to the railroad station in Asino, a trip of about ten miles. On the way to Asino it began to snow again. This time the snowflakes were big and fluffy and covered everything in sight. The snow fell quietly but steadily, as if to say "you are leaving just in time!" When we reached Asino the ground was covered with a blanket several inches thick.

The Asino railroad station was a one-room, shabby log cabin with a hot water faucet to make tea if one had it—otherwise you just drank hot water. The elderly station-master was shabby too. He scurried around telling everyone in the crowded station that the train to Novosibirsk, the hub for this region, should arrive the next day. When night fell we bedded down on the station floor.

The train arrived the next morning. To our pleasant surprise, it was a regular passenger train with seats and windows. We had assumed that we would yet again be traveling in boxcars. Moshe and I picked seats next to the window, and we even had a folding table between us.

The passage to Novosibirsk was comfortable and warm in comparison to the trip from Lubomel to Siberia. I was glued to the window watching the unfolding scenery of the taiga. It seemed as if the train was rolling inside a tunnel carved through an endless and solid mass of trees. To my young eyes, the giant green pines covered with a sprinkling of early snow looked as though they had been painted by an artist with a magic brush. Again we passed boxcars filled with prisoners, who peered at us through tiny windows covered with barbed-wire. We rolled past places with which we were already familiar from our trip to Siberia, but this time we greeted them with hope in our hearts.

In the morning we arrived in Novosibirsk. As we approached, the tracks began to branch out into ever-widening steel paths leading to many different places. We finally stopped in front of the main terminal, a long, white, clean-looking building. The station was bustling with soldiers returning—and refugees fleeing—from the war with Germany. We settled in one of the corners of the great hall to await our next move. But we had not yet decided where to go.

Novosibirsk was restricted for security reasons, so we were not allowed to leave the terminal. Moshe and I set out to see if we could find some food in the station, as the latkes had all been eaten. We discovered that the interior of the terminal, like the one in Kiev, was decorated with statues of various Soviet heroes. Huge chandeliers hung from the ceiling and mosaics and paintings adorned the walls. Soon we came across a restaurant, but the workers did not allow us to enter. We could smell the food, however, and when a crowd of people entered we squeezed inside unnoticed. Moshe and I grabbed some leftover bread from the tables and stuffed our mouths and pockets with it, but we were quickly chased out. In the meantime Papa and Wolf sneaked into town to buy some food.

My parents decided that we should go south. There was war in the west, and Siberia was to the east and north, so we really had no other choice. Besides, the south was warm.

My father booked passage to the city of Tashkent in Uzbekistan, more than a thousand miles to the southwest of Novosibirsk on the other side of the Republic of Kazakhstan. My parents did not tell us why they chose Tashkent. The only thing I knew about it from my studies in school was that during the Russian Revolution it was referred to as *Tashkent gorod khlebny*—"Tashkent, the Bread City." That sounded promising!

Most of the available trains were reserved for the war effort, so we had to wait at the station for several days before we could board a train going south. When our train finally came, we once again settled into a passenger car permeated with the smell of locomotive steam and smoke. The others in our car were mostly Ukrainians and Russians—old men, women, and children fleeing the raging war in the west. These refugees brought with them horrible tales about the atrocities of the Germans. At the very start of the war we had heard something similar, but these new tales of murder were unbelievable. We thought this might be a case of Soviet propaganda—for how could the most civilized nation in Europe behave so barbarically? Yet talking to these people made me think of the loved ones we had left behind in Poland. We had not heard from any of them since we left in 1939. The women said that some of their husbands and sons had joined the resistance. Listening to their stories, I too began to dream of hiding in the forest and fighting Germans.

We traveled south into Kazakhstan, famous for its endless, wind-blown steppes. The landscape was flat and monotonous. Occasionally we passed small mud dwellings stuck on top of parched land. The weather became milder and sunny, and we opened the car windows to get some warm fresh air. In Semipalatinsk, the first large city in Kazakhstan, the train stopped long enough for my father to run to town to obtain some food. While in Semipalatinsk I saw several trainloads of Red Army units ready to be shipped to the front lines to fight the Germans.

Papa and Wolf made it back to the station just before we pulled out. My mother was a nervous wreck by then, because she was certain that they were going to miss the train.

We continued south to Alma-Ata, the capital of Kazakhstan. The land along our route was flat all the way to the horizon. Alma-Ata was not like the other Russian cities we had seen, in that it had a distinctly oriental atmosphere. The population was a mixture of Tartars, Uzbeks, Mongols, and other ethnic groups. Because it was Soviet policy to promote the settlement of ethnic Russians in the various non-Russian republics, many Russians lived in Kazakhstan as well. The Kazakhs, famous for their horsemanship and nomadic lifestyle, are Muslims—but the Soviets, being communists, did not officially acknowledge this fundamental fact. Many of the natives still lived in traditional dwellings called yurts, which are circular tents made of felt or animal skins.

Alma-Ata was spread out over a wide area covered mostly with low, flat-roofed, white buildings. The majestic snow-capped peaks of the Himalayas provided a striking backdrop.

When we arrived in Alma-Ata, the conductor informed us that our train would be going no farther. He advised us to check with the terminal dispatcher to make other arrangements. We got off the train and settled down in the terminal. The dispatcher informed us that the next train bound for Tashkent wouldn't arrive for several hours, and would be a freight train. Many of the Russian passengers protested, but by now we were used to traveling in freight cars.

With extra time on our hands we decided to go to town for provisions. We asked some of the locals where we could buy food and were directed to the town's bazaar. It was a short walk there, and as we approached we could hear

the vendors shouting out their wares. The bazaar was a large area full of little stalls. The vendors sat on the ground peddling dried fruits, vegetables, pita
bread, and many other products. It was a noisy place, and the prices were extremely high. My father and mother bought such food as they could afford. I
don't know how much money my father had saved in Siberia, but it could not
have been much. I had the feeling that they were already running low on
money. Pretending to be a customer, I tasted some of the dried fruit at one of
the stalls. The fruit was delicious, although I have no idea what kind it was
since I had never tasted anything like it before. But I did discover that I could
satisfy my hunger for a while by sampling fruit from the various stalls.

Several hours later our train arrived. We boarded one of the box cars, in
which there were already some other families. Soon we were on our way to
Tashkent, the capital of Uzbekistan.

We arrived in Tashkent at night. It certainly did not look like the City of
Bread to me. The town was dark and foreboding, with only a few lights burning here and there. Perhaps this was why my parents decided against disem-
barking, even though Tashkent had been our original destination.

We stayed on the train all night, and in the morning we were told the train
would go as far as Samarkand, a city about 150 miles to the southwest. After
some deliberation, the adults elected to go on to Samarkand. But that was not
the last that Tashkent would see of our family. I learned later that my father's
cousins Hendl and Judith had lived there for several years during the war. After the war Hendl immigrated to the United States, and her sister Judith immigrated to Israel.

As we continued south to Samarkand the weather became much warmer.
The little villages we passed consisted of mud huts and small dwellings constructed of red clay reinforced with straw. Every now and then we saw people on horseback, donkeys, and even camels. It was the first time we had ever
seen either camels or donkeys. The horses were much smaller than the ones I
was used to. It turned out they were Mongolians, the same kind of horses that
Genghis Khan and his descendants rode on when their armies conquered Asia
and much of the eastern part of Europe. I do not recall seeing any paved high-
ways or streets on the way to Samarkand.

The national dress of the Uzbeks is very colorful, with delicately embroidered shirts, long coats, and baggy pants. The people I saw covered their
heads with round embroidered caps, and on their feet they wore sandals or
high boots. The females wore flowing robes and homemade jewelry composed of all sorts of coins. Some women wore sandals but most of them were
barefoot. All the males carried curved daggers crafted with silver inlays or
some other kind of shiny metal. I was told by the locals that sometimes they
use these daggers to settle disputes. It all seemed strange and exotic to me.

Every time we came to a new town, my parents had to decide whether to stop there. They hoped to settle in a place that was neither a large city nor a small town. The big cities were flooded with refugees, and the small towns, they thought, were not capable of supplying essential social services.

About fifty kilometers from Samarkand we stopped at a town called Krasnogvardeysk. Papa and Wolf got off the train to scout around and make some inquiries. There was a place for Papa to work in a small shoe factory, and in general the place seemed to have some possibilities. In addition the town looked more European than Oriental, as the majority of its inhabitants seemed to be Russian. In spite of all this, my father and uncle decided that we would first see what the larger city of Samarkand had to offer.

Samarkand is a very old city with a rich history. Famous for its silk and cotton production, it was situated on the ancient trade route between China and the Middle East. It was conquered by Alexander the Great and Genghis Khan, and was the capital of the empire of Tamerlane. Yet it turned out to be just as inhospitable to refugees as any other big city. Displaced people were everywhere, including families with children and old men and women. People bedded down in the rail station, on the streets, and in hallways. Every available space was crammed with them. And they came from all over. They spoke Russian, Polish, Yiddish, Ukrainian, Uzbek, and other languages that were unknown to me.

We looked everywhere in Samarkand for a place to rent, but nothing was to be found. Exhausted, hungry, and filthy—for we had not washed since we left Sukhoy-Log—we flopped down along a mud fence on a side street not far from the rail station. Papa and Wolf had to rethink their decision to come to Samarkand, as it was obviously a bad choice.

My parents were constantly fighting against feelings of hopelessness and despair. My mother cried often during these difficult days, and my father was unusually irritable. As for me, I was now fourteen and beginning to notice pretty girls. But I was very self-conscious and shy because of my shabby, ill-fitting clothes, which were the same ones I was wearing when we left Poland. I was also dirty, and I stank.

As on our trip to Siberia, the local health department set up a disinfecting station for refugees. At the station we undressed, put nametags on our clothes, and turned them in. Our clothing was then placed in a huge steel tank that looked like a steamer except that it generated dry heat. About fifteen minutes later our clothes were returned. They were hot and scorched in spots, and still dirty—but they were now free of lice.

After two more days on the street, we boarded a train to go back to Krasnogvardeysk. Krasnogvardeysk, we found, was peaceful and quiet compared to Samarkand. The small, red-brick railway station was shaded from the midday heat by big trees. Opposite the station was the marketplace, which was full of hustling vendors and people milling around. Everything was outrageously expensive, as inflation was rampant in Uzbekistan. The government had instituted fixed pricing, but no one seemed to pay any attention to the law.

Moshe and I were told to stay at the station and watch our belongings while our parents went to look for a place to rent. When they returned they were smiling. We picked up our belongings and walked to our new home, about four blocks from the station. The twisting streets on the way to our new place were lined with mud-walled cottages with large courtyards, which is the characteristic architecture of the area. Occasionally one would see a European-style home inhabited by Russians. The courtyards of most of the cottages had a water-well and wash-basin plus a round mud oven—the kind in which you bake pita bread by pasting the dough on the inside wall.

Our new home was a U-shaped, low-slung duplex constructed of mud and straw. In the center of the U between the two wings were two doors made of rough wood. One door led to our lodging and the other belonged to our neighbors, the Zlobov family. Both apartments had the same floor plan. As you entered there was a small kitchen that was bare except for a clay wood-burning stove. The kitchen led to another small room that contained a table, two wooden benches, and an iron-framed double bed with a straw mattress. The floor was clay dirt with patches here and there where it had been repaired.

Olga, our landlady, lived in our half of the duplex along with us. She was an attractive young woman of about twenty-five. Her newly married husband, she told us, had been drafted into the cavalry and shipped out to fight the Germans. But he was now recuperating in a hospital because of an infected horse bite on his hand. Olga seemed to be very lonely and wanted us to move in with her until she left for Siberia to live with her parents.

We made our bedding on the floor in the kitchen and tried to stay out of the way as much as possible. Olga offered Moshe and me part of her double bed, but we refused. We got along very well with her, and she and Mama quickly became good friends. They talked, cooked, and went to market together. But only a few weeks after we moved in, Olga's passage came through and she left for Siberia to live with her parents. Olga's sister-in-law, who lived about ten kilometers away, was to collect the rent from us.

Our neighbor, whom we nicknamed "Babushka," had two children. Fedya was about eighteen, and Manya was a pretty, blue-eyed Russian blond. Babushka was much younger than she looked. We guessed that she was in her late thirties or early forties, but her kerchief-covered head and wrinkled face made her look grandmotherly. She worked in a slaughter house that supplied beef for the Red Army. Babushka apparently did not have a husband; at least, she never mentioned one.

The Zlobovs also had a watchdog—part bulldog and part something else—called Sasha. Sasha was chained to a steel cable that allowed him to roam across the entire front of the house. He was a vicious animal. Sasha once bit a beggar several times before Babushka and I were able to drag him away from the man. Sasha was never formally fed. Babushka turned him loose once a day to fend for himself, and he always seemed to turn up something to eat. One day I saw him eating a tomato and I wondered where in Krasnogvardeysk he had ever found such a rare treat.

Fedya was getting ready to go to the army and had little to do with us kids. But I liked Manya very much, and we became good friends. Sometimes we would walk down the street holding hands and singing Russian songs. Other times we would go out into the fields to collect tumbleweeds for the cook stove. Our duplex was on the edge of town, and sometimes the tumbleweeds blew right up against the house.

Once in a while Babushka brought extra meat from the slaughterhouse and invited Moshe and me in for dinner. We greatly appreciated her hospitality, as meat was very expensive and available only on the black market.

Although the general economic situation in town was poor, my father's resourcefulness made it bearable for my family. Papa got a job in a small shoe factory manufacturing boots for the Red Army, but his salary could not buy much on the black market. Bread was rationed at 600 grams (1.3 lbs.) per day, and only working people received rations. So Papa also worked at home in the evening, making boots that he could sell on the black market. This sort of thing was against the law, but he was encouraged by some NKVD officials who wanted specially-made boots. The black market was fueled by local farmers. Every time the government tried to implement price controls, the farmers would withhold goods from the market and people would go hungry. Finally the officials looked the other way, as there was apparently no punishment that could persuade the locals to give in.

In order to supplement my diet I used to go to the market and help the Uzbeks sell some of their wares. In return they would let me eat some of their dried fruit or vegetables, and I sometimes "sampled" the food as well. On occasion a vendor would send me home with a bag full of dried fruit, and my mother would then prepare a sugarless compote.

The school term was at hand and Mama wanted Moshe and me to enroll. She even found second-hand books for me that I could use in the seventh grade. I liked the idea of school but my heart was not in it. I had no clothes that fit and I felt that I would be unable to concentrate because of my constant hunger. So I urged my mother to let me attend a trade school in a sugar factory that was under construction and needed to create a supply of skilled workers. The factory was starting six-month classes for training in various fields. The schedule was half a day of theory and half a day of practice. I pointed out to my parents that as a trainee I would be entitled to 600 grams of bread a day—plus food in the cafeteria, where they served horsemeat for lunch.

My mother reluctantly gave in and I enrolled in a course to study electro-mechanics. In class we learned about various sorts of electric motors. In the afternoon we assisted skilled workers. After signing up, I received a ration card for bread and was allowed to eat in the cafeteria. The meal was a bowl of horsemeat stew with cabbage, potatoes, and bread. It was not enough to last all day, but it kept me from starving. All too often, however, the cafeteria did not receive supplies. On such days the cafeteria was closed and I had to make it on my ration of one thick slice of moist bread. I later found out why the bread was so moist and seemingly under-baked. The baker was obliged to supply a given number of kilograms to a distribution center, and by making the bread heavy he could steal the extra flour and sell bread on the black market.

The construction site for the sugar factory was near the marketplace, so I did not have far to go to get to work. The class started at eight A.M. sharp and was held in the chief engineer's office. Absenteeism was rampant, perhaps because many of the students suffered from malnutrition and disease. There were no benches or tables, so we sat on the floor and took notes while listening to lectures delivered by various plant supervisors. There were no books. The instructors used a blackboard and sometimes brought in equipment for demonstration. I found the subjects very interesting and did my best to absorb as much as I could from the lectures. In the afternoons, we were shown how to use drill presses and how to cut and form steel and sheet metal. We were also taught blacksmithing and electric-arc welding. We were lectured on safety precautions, but hard hats and gloves were not available to us. Safety glasses, however, could be checked out from the supply office.

After some time in training I made two knives from a discarded steel blade. One was about ten inches long and the other was about six inches. I riveted two aluminum handles onto the blades and fashioned two scabbards. I was very proud of my accomplishment. Since most Uzbeks carried a knife, I felt that I should have one also. One of my neighbors down the street, a Tartar, saw the bigger knife and offered to buy it from me. I sold it to him, but kept the small knife for myself and carried it on me at all times.

The knife proved handy. There was a bully about my age who kept harassing Moshe and me every time we passed his house. On one occasion we were returning from the marketplace and he shouted out a rhyming taunt: *Yevrey,*

Yevrey, nye pugay golubyey ("Jew, Jew, don't scare the pigeons"). I had had enough of the pest, so I pulled my knife and moved towards him, pointing at my throat to show him where I was going to cut him. The boy began to scream and ran into his house. From then on he left us alone.

The work at the plant was interesting, but sometimes we would amuse ourselves by hiding in the big steel tanks. The bosses would then scold us, complaining that "they send us kids to do a man's job." But my supervisor, Tovarishch Sacharoff, was always nice to me. Whenever I told him I was hungry he would let me go to the bazaar to try to get my hands on some fruit. Our hunger led us students to try some strange things. Once, one of the students found a turtle and took it to the forging furnace in the blacksmith shop to fry it, but he was chased away by the blacksmith.

The plant construction site was being excavated in order to prepare a foundation to hold heavy machinery. This heavy work was done by prisoners under the watchful eyes of armed guards and dogs provided by the NKVD. The prisoners were housed in special barracks built just outside the plant grounds, so there would be no need to transport them to work. The barracks were surrounded by a ten-foot stockade made of pine logs topped with bared wire. There were also watchtowers for the guards. A big double-door gate and a small door next to it were the only ways in and out of the camp. Every morning the prisoners were marched into the construction site under heavy guard, and every evening they were marched back out. The prisoners did their job using only shovels and wheelbarrows. The excavation area, which in some places was only a few yards from our work station, was restricted to guards and inmates, and posted signs warned "Unauthorized Persons Will Be Shot."

A couple of times I witnessed an attempted escape. The siren was activated and the dogs were turned loose to chase after the prisoners. At such times, the guards ordered all prisoners to sit down on the ground and fired warning shots over their heads. In our shop we would be instructed to take cover. The dogs generally caught up with the escapees, and when they were hauled back the guards would beat them with clubs or with their rifle butts.

Once three convicts escaped but only two came back. I have no idea what happened to the third prisoner. On another occasion a civilian in our plant scolded the guards for beating an inmate. The man was promptly arrested for his trouble, but later released.

I once got a look at the inside of the prison camp. I had to use the toilet, and I stupidly walked through the small door next to the gate looking for a place to go. As I entered the courtyard of the prison an officer approached me and demanded to know what I was doing. When I told him, he shouted: "Get out of here! Go look for a toilet somewhere else!" Then I caught sight of the inmates peering out of their cells. I ran out of the camp as fast as I could.

The fall was coming to an end. It was getting cold, but it was nothing compared to Siberia. Occasionally we had a sprinkling of snow that melted a day or two later, only to be replaced by sticky red clay or mud. Our apartment had no heating other than the little cook stove, which didn't help much. But the weather was mild and I don't remember ever being chilled.

I completed my training program in January of 1942 and received a certificate stating that I was a *razryad vtoroy*—electrician's helper, second grade. They misspelled my name and instead of Ezya Goldman it said Ezya Goldenman. I brought this to the attention of Tovarishch Sacharoff so he took a pen, crossed out the "en," and said: *Tyepyer khorosho*, "Now it's good." I was assigned to work with an experienced electrician so that I would learn more about the trade on the job. We had to manufacture many of the components and parts ourselves, which is why we were classified as "electro-mechanics."

The radio was constantly broadcasting reports about the victories of the Red Army. Over and over, we heard that "our glorious and brave Red Army is delivering mortal blows to the German snake." There were posters all over town depicting Soviet soldiers overrunning evil-looking Germans in their trenches. In spite of these claims of victory, however, refugees kept pouring in from the west.

As more and more refugees arrived, the troubles that we had encountered in the big cities became evident in Krasnogvardeysk as well. Food and sanitation became big problems, to the point where people began to die from starvation and disease. The government-rationed supplies dried up, and many times the distribution store had nothing but bare shelves. The few supplies that the Uzbek farmers were able to bring to market were absurdly expensive. Even black market food was hard to come by. Whatever food became available was earmarked for the Red Army.

Eventually, it became customary for a cart to drive down the streets in the morning for the purpose of picking up and hauling off people who had died during the night.

When a person begins to starve, he can think only about how to obtain food. When he manages to come across a piece of bread, he watches every crumb. When we did get our rations of bread, Mama made sure that it was divided in precisely equal portions, so as to not cheat anyone of their share.

Mother managed to cook soup every day, but it was more like water than what you would call soup. Bless her memory, she went all over town trying to scrape up a potato or anything else she could use for the soup. She had no fat or oil or salt for seasoning, but our stomachs felt full after we ate. On rare occasions Babushka would give us a bone with some meat on it and then the soup tasted much better. But Babushka was taking a big risk herself because she was stealing meat from the slaughter house.

Olga' sister-in-law worked in a bakery in a small village near our town, and she always brought our family two loaves of bread when she came to collect the rent. We learned from her that her brother, who was Olga's husband, had been killed in the war. This woman invited us to come to her village for a while, saying that she would fatten us up with bread. My brother and I took her up on her invitation. We stayed in her cottage, which was similar to ours but had a clear brook flowing through the yard. In the distance we could see the snow-capped Himalayas. Moshe and I stayed there several days and ate as much bread as we could.

We found another source of food when the manager of a slaughter-house gave me permission to collect blood. Every day I came with a bucket, and as an animal was slaughtered I placed my bucket under its throat and filled it with blood. My mother then cooked the blood in a skillet. Prepared in this way, blood tastes something like liver, and looks like liver or lung depending on how long it is cooked. My father and Moshe loved it, but Mama and I could not develop a taste for it. Maybe I would have liked it if it had been seasoned with salt. But it didn't matter because after a couple of weeks there was no more blood, as there were no more cows to be slaughtered.

Good hygiene was impossible in Krasnogvardeysk. There was no running water, the outhouses were not tended to, and there was no soap to do laundry or wash up with. Toothpaste was unheard of. A person could pick up lice by just brushing up against someone on the street or public place.

I eventually came down with a high fever, which turned out to be the result of malaria. I did not go to work and no one seemed to care. It was just as well, as I don't remember ever getting a salary from the plant. I was alternately cold and hot from the fever, and no amount of blankets could keep me warm. Mama tried to make me feel comfortable as best as she could, especially when I was hallucinating.

There was a clinic in town but the number of sick people exceeded its bed capacity. The sick were put in the hallways and on the floor. I was better off staying at home even though we had no proper medicines. Out of desperation Mama tried some local folk-remedies consisting of herbs.

Somehow the crisis passed and I came out of it. After a while, however, my father became sick with high fever and was laid up in bed. Mother tended to his needs and again tried her best to make him feel comfortable, but things got worse and he lost his appetite for food. We knew than that his condition was serious. When he developed dark blotches on his body, Mama began to suspect typhoid. She took him to the clinic and he was indeed diagnosed with typhoid fever. The clinic quarantined him and put him up in a room with others who were also suffering from typhoid. Mama went to see him every day. Since she wasn't allowed to enter his room, she had to be content with observing him through a window.

Before Papa went to the clinic, I had eaten some food from which he had taken only a bite or two. This proved to be a serious mistake. Mama and I were on an errand near the sugar plant when I began to feel ill. I sat down under a tree while Mama went about her business. Sitting under the tree I began to feel dizzy and numb, my head started to spin, and I passed out. When Mama came out and found me slumped over she screamed for help. Luckily a nearby building had a first aid room. A male nurse there revived me and diagnosed me as having typhoid fever.

Mama took me at once to the clinic where my father was quarantined, and upon her insistence I was placed in the same room with him. Since the room was full, they put me on a mattress on the floor. I was nauseous but otherwise not feeling very bad. Papa, however, was drifting in and out of consciousness. Here, too, there was no medicine available. Many patients died while in the clinic.

Mama sold some of her possessions to obtain some medicine on the black market. A female doctor came in to administer the medicine to my father, which she did by injection. After that, his condition started to improve. Like Papa, my temperature shot up and I had some bouts of convulsive vomiting, but then I too began to feel better.

My father and I left the quarantine at the same time. In retrospect I can't help wondering if we were diagnosed correctly. After all, no blood samples were taken from either of us. In fact, I don't believe there was a laboratory anywhere nearby that was capable of analyzing blood samples. I did have dark blotches on my body, however, and that was one symptom of typhoid.

Mama and Moshe never contracted any kind of serious disease while in the U.S.S.R. Their immune systems must have been stronger than ours.

It was the spring of 1942, and after the mild winter everything was in bloom. I was back working in the plant and things more or less became routine. The food situation had its ups and downs, but even in the best of times there was never quite enough to eat.

The war in the west began to take a turn for the better. The advance of the Germans into the Soviet Union was stopped near Moscow and Stalingrad by a Red Army counter-offensive. The allied forces—including England and her colonies, aided by American supplies—exerted significant pressure on the Germans as well. In the meantime the Polish government-in-exile began to form a Polish army that was to be equipped by England. Since a large segment of the Polish citizenry was in the Soviet Union, a major campaign was being carried out, with the approval of the Soviet government, to mobilize young men into a Polish fighting force. I took some pride in being Polish and began to wear an old Polish army hat. Now, I dreamt, we would take revenge on those Germans and make them pay dearly for their foul deeds. But it was childish of me to think that way, as I was soon to find out.

As the saying goes, "when it rains it pours." As if I had not had enough sickness already, I came down with a bad case of dysentery. I may have picked it up by drinking water out of an open barrel at the plant, or perhaps by eating some unwashed apples. For over a month I could not hold any nourishment, and I had blood in my stools. The clinic would not admit me, as they said there was no room and no medicine for dysentery.

I was getting dehydrated and began to look like a skeleton. When I looked in a mirror I could hardly recognize myself. I felt much worse than when I had typhoid or malaria. My stomach cramps were excruciating, and I also developed a fever and became delirious. Mama was constantly asking God for help, and Moshe and Papa seemed very worried. But my mother did not give up. She walked all over town asking for help. One day she came home with some medicine that she obtained from a woman, also a refugee, who claimed that she was a doctor.

The medicine—I have no idea what it was—came in a little bottle. I was ordered by my mother to drink all of it. It tasted like concentrated lemon juice and puckered my whole mouth. When it reached my stomach, all hell's fire descended into my poor insides. I screamed in pain and collapsed on the dirt floor. But when I awoke, I sensed that I was going to be alright.

A few days later I began to improve. Mama was somehow able to find a chicken egg, and she served it to me soft-boiled. That egg—the first one I had eaten since we left the Ukraine—was delicious. When I regained enough strength to walk again, my mother offered a prayer of thanks to our Almighty Father in Heaven and Master of the Universe for returning her son to health. I will never forget my mother's devotion and endless effort to make me well. There is no question in my mind that had it not been for her tireless care, I would have died.

The process of recruiting Polish citizens to form a Polish army was being carried out in various districts throughout the southern republics of the Soviet Union. I sometimes saw trains loaded with Polish recruits passing our town on their way west. There was speculation that the recruits were leaving the U.S.S.R. on their way to Persia (now called Iran) or Africa, but nobody seemed to know for certain.

The rule was that the immediate family of a draftee was entitled to leave the U.S.S.R. as well. We all wanted to leave, so my father made a decision to try to join up. After all, he had served in the artillery of the Polish army only fourteen years earlier, and he felt that the army needed men with his kind of training and experience. The recruiting station was in Samarkand, only about an hour away by train. But Papa came back from Samarkand bitterly disappointed. He was turned down, although I never learned the reason why. Papa thought it was because he was Jewish. I later learned that other Jews from the

U.S.S.R. were accepted into the Polish army, including my uncle Karp as well as Menachem Begin, who went on to become Prime Minister of Israel. But it is possible that the recruiter in Samarkand was an anti-Semite. It may also be that Papa was past the age for recruitment, as he was then thirty-five years old.

There were many Polish children in the U.S.S.R. whose parents had died or were missing, and someone needed to care for them. Thus orphanages were organized with the intention of shipping out the children along with the new recruits. One such orphanage, with some fifty children, was established in Krasnogvardeysk. The orphanage had a regular staff with a female director, and was part of the office of the Polish ambassador. My brother and I applied, claiming to be orphans. My parents figured that if we could somehow get out of the Soviet Union our chances for survival would be better. They also reasoned that they might be able to join us later.

My brother was accepted by the orphanage, but I was rejected for being over the age limit of twelve. This created a dilemma, since my parents had planned that I would look out for Moshe. If I could not go, then Moshe would also have to stay. However, my father knew the Polish ambassador, as he was one of Papa's black-market customers. Papa promised the ambassador a pair of fancy boots at no charge if he would somehow arrange for me to get into the orphanage. The ambassador accepted the deal and told Papa that my name would be on the exit list at the point of departure.

One day we were told to get ready to leave for the station, as the orphans were going to Tashkent. I ran to tell my parents that we were moving out. Our departure was heartbreaking. My mother clung to me and would not let go. She cried the whole time. My father gave me some money just in case I had to come back, and told me to look out for my brother. Other families were going through the same sad ritual.

Finally Mama had to let go of us. The train was ready to depart. Moshe cried terribly and did not want to leave our parents. We wondered if we would ever meet again. It was not until I became a parent myself that I understood how my mother and father must have felt.

My name was not on the list of orphans, but I traveled to the Tashkent concentration area with the permission of the ambassador. The director of the orphanage knew about this, but she did not like it. Once or twice she remarked that there was trouble in store for me. I did not understand what she meant, but I did my best to stay out of her way. It was clear that she did not like me. I was not the only one in this situation, for there were two other Jewish boys my age whose inclusion on the list was also uncertain.

The concentration area for our final departure from the U.S.S.R. was an open field with some low-slung trees and a clear, winding brook. We were not the only group there, as there were children and adults from other areas as well. No one knew who was in charge, so there was mass confusion. Even there, some army recruiters were registering people for the military. The only water available was from the brook, which we drank and used to wash our clothing. Moshe shared with me some of the food he was given by the orphanage, but I also had to buy some food. After several days I ran out of money.

Because I had no idea how much longer we would be at the camp, I decided to go back to Krasnogvardeysk to get some more money from my parents. I could not rely on Moshe's food because there was hardly enough for one, much less for two. Since I was broke, my only option was to ride the train as a stow-away. I knew that my plans would be ruined if the conductor caught me.

I boarded the train and told Moshe that I would be back in a day or so. When I got on the train I met a couple of boys my age who were also planning to ride for free. We immediately became comrades in arms. One of the boys suggested that we design a document in Polish and imprint a Polish coin on it to make it look like it had an official stamp. About halfway to Krasnogvardeysk the conductor made the rounds and stopped one of the boys. The boy had no choice but to try out his fake document. Needless to say he failed to fool the conductor, who told him that he would be thrown off the train at the next stop. I was observing all this from a safe distance and decided that it was time to move. I hid between the cars by holding on to a railing while perching on the outside of the train. After the conductor passed by I climbed back on the train. I never learned what happened to my co-conspirators.

I arrived home safely and gave my parents the surprise of their lives. They were very glad to see me and they wanted to know where Moshe was. I explained the situation. My father gave me some more money and told me to go back at once so that I would not miss my chance to leave the Soviet Union. We went back to the station and fortunately there was a freight train getting ready to leave for Tashkent. Papa bribed the conductor and he agreed to allow me on one of the freight cars. I said good-by again and was off to Tashkent.

The next day, I arrived in Tashkent at sunrise. I was just in time, for the whole camp was up and moving to the main terminal. I connected with our group and found Moshe. Was he glad to see me!

We all walked as a group to the rail station, the older children leading the younger ones. Moshe and I held the hands of two little kids. I was somewhat anxious about what might happen if my name was not called. Intermingled with us were many women who hoped to get on board by claiming that their husbands had been drafted and had already left on another train. But as far as

I could tell, these women did not have any documentation to back up their claims.

I anticipated much confusion at the station and I was right. I dragged Moshe and some kids as close as possible to a car. The cars were filled with draftees dressed in British uniforms. Each door was guarded by one of the soldiers to make sure that the train would not be boarded in a disorderly manner. I told Moshe that if my name was not called and I didn't get on, I would take another train and catch up with him later.

We waited next to the train for what seemed like an eternity. The ambassador had the list in his hands, and with it the fate of all those waiting to depart. The crowd suddenly grew silent when the ambassador climbed up on a loading platform and began calling out names. It seemed like he was never going to get to us. Finally I heard "Mikhal Goldman," and I pushed Moshe forward. Then I heard "Yuzef Goldman," and I too got on the train. Surprisingly, my father's name was also called, but not my mother's. Of course, that was irrelevant because my parents were not there. I was confused as to why the ambassador changed "Moshe" to "Mikhal" and "Israel" to "Yuzef." Later, when we were safely out of the Soviet Union, I did some investigating and was told that the Polish officials routinely "Polishized" Jewish names. Why they did this is beyond me, especially since Mikhal and Yuzef are also Hebrew names for Michael and Joseph. So they traded Hebrew names for Hebrew names.

In the confusion at the railroad station, many of the thousands of people who were present were not called even though their names were legitimately on the list. Some of these people stretched themselves out on the tracks in front of the steam engine, but the police dragged them off and the train set out. It was a pitiful sight to behold, but all the same I breathed a sigh of relief when we got underway. In hindsight, I believe that my mother could somehow have boarded the train along with my father had they both been there.

When the director of the orphanage saw me on the train, she exclaimed angrily: "How in the devil did you get on?" I told her I was on the list. She gave me a nasty look and stormed off. I resolved then to stay out of her way at all costs.

Our destination was the port Krasnovodsk on the eastern shore of the Caspian Sea, about a thousand miles west of Tashkent. I knew that the train would have to pass our little town of Krasnogvardeysk. I hoped that somehow I could contact my parents, especially since Papa's place of work was very close to the station. But I had no way to alert them to our arrival.

In the morning we arrived in Krasnogvardeysk, and the train even stopped for a short while. I stuck my head out of the window hoping to see at least one of my parents, but no such luck. I had some leftover money that I had hoped to return to my father, and I also wanted to share with my parents a bag full of chocolates that the soldiers had given us. I spotted a friend of the family and called his name; he ran over and I gave him the money and chocolates. I watched him run to my father's workplace, and then I saw Papa rush out of the shop. At the same moment, however, the train began to move. Papa had only enough time to wave goodbye to us.

Moshe and I had tears in our eyes. We did not know if we would ever see our father again.

Our journey took us across the Uzbek and Turkmen republics of the U.S.S.R., and through the cities of Samarkand, Buchara, and Aschabad into Krasnovodsk. The trip took about forty-eight hours. The scenery was desolate, just as it was on our way to Uzbekistan one year earlier. But the passenger cars were comfortable, and the soldiers on the train showered us with all kinds of chocolates and cookies. I was ecstatic, and I'm sure that the other children felt the same way. Those treats were part of the rations supplied by the British. There was also plenty of white bread and canned meat. After almost three years of near-starvation, we finally had more than enough to eat.

In spite of my efforts to hide from the director of the orphanage, she spotted me once again and demanded that I show her proof of my permit for this trip. I showed her my pass, but only from a distance—and I would not let it out of my grip. I did not trust her and feared that she would tear it up if she got hold of it. That infuriated her. She turned red in her face and promised to get even with me and kick me off the train at the first chance. This was exactly what I feared.

From then on, Moshe and the other children warned me whenever she approached. I was determined that no one was going to get me off this fantastic train full of chocolates! Fortunately, our paths did not cross again until we reached Krasnovodsk.

In Krasnovodsk the train stopped several hundred yards from the station and we were told to get off. To our right was the low skyline of the city, and in front of us the shimmering blue sea. I had never seen a sea before, and I could not take my eyes off this vast expanse of water that stretched all the way to the horizon.

A jerk on my sleeve, courtesy of my brother, brought me back to my immediate surroundings. The whole group was directed to a treeless spot near the shore. We cleared away some rocks and pebbles and used our blankets to make tents in order to shield ourselves from the oppressive heat of the sun. For what seemed like the thousandth time since we had left Poland, we settled down to wait. As usual, nobody seemed to know what was happening or how long we would have to sit there by the sea.

Our camping spot was terribly hot, and the blankets afforded little relief from the sun. The only other living thing we could see was a donkey standing near a shack about a mile away. Everyone was thirsty. But then I had an idea: why should one be thirsty next to the sea? I walked down to the water for a dip and a drink. How was I to know that sea water was salty? I must have been asleep when they taught us that in school.

The first swallow of water made me gag and see stars. I coughed and spat for the rest of the day. What is worse, the sea water made me even more thirsty. I had to have some sweet water. I figured the shack in the distance might have water. If there was a donkey, then there must be some people nearby.

I walked to the shack and knocked on the door. A middle-aged Turkman came out and asked me what I wanted. I told him that I had drunk sea water and would he please give me some water to quench my thirst? He laughed heartily. I suppose he thought my situation was funny. But then he took me to his bucket behind the shack and let me drink from it. After I had had my fill, I had another idea: would he bring us water if I gave him some chocolates? I don't know if he had ever eaten any chocolate, but he certainly knew what it was. He told me that drinking water had to be brought in from town, but was willing to give us whatever water he had in exchange for the chocolates. We sealed the deal with a handshake.

The Turkman loaded up the donkey with two barrels of water and we walked over to the camp. I collected the chocolates from the kids and we made a trade that satisfied everyone.

One afternoon Moshe and I were resting under our blanket pup-tent with our feet sticking out. Two boys who were the director's personal servants walked by our tent carrying a load of drift wood to kindle a fire for the director. As they came by, one of them purposely stepped on Moshe's ankle and twisted it badly. Moshe screamed in pain while the two boys stood there and laughed. That infuriated me. I grabbed one of the pieces of driftwood and clubbed the living daylights out of both of them. They ran to the director with tears in their eyes, screaming "The Jews beat us up!" The director came running over. Her face was red and she was shaking with anger. She exclaimed repeatedly "I knew I would have trouble with you Goldmans!" When she raised her hand to slap my brother, I jumped in between them and said: "Just you try!" She looked at me in disbelief, but eventually she backed off.

After that episode neither the director nor her helpers bothered us again. In any case her duty was now done, as the NKVD oversaw the transports out of the U.S.S.R.

The following day, two men from the NKVD came around and ordered everyone to turn in any Soviet currency they might have. After that, we were marched two-by-two towards the docks to board a freighter for the trip across the Caspian Sea. At the entrance to the ship two Russian policemen held a blanket and again told everyone to put their Soviet currency in it. No one checked us for any passes or permits to leave. I had already disposed of my electrician's rating certificate from the sugar plant, fearing that if I were searched I might be sent back. All the Russian policemen did was count the number of people boarding the ship.I didn't know what to expect next, but we were soon to find out.

Papa (in army uniform), Bob, and Mama. Chelm, Poland, 1928.

Mama, Moshe, Papa, and Bob. Chelm, 1932.

Bob and Moshe in a city park. Chelm, 1934.

*Mama, Papa, Bob, Moshe, and Grandmother Naomi
in a city park. Chelm, 1937.*

Bob and Moshe in their school uniforms. Chelm, 1938.

Moshe and Bob at Mikveh Israel, 1943.

*Bob's photo for his British
Mandate identification card, 1945.*

Moshe Olek, Asher Halpern, Moshe Butman and Bob Golan. Tel Aviv, 1946.

Moshe (in Settlement Police uniform) and Bob.
Tel Aviv, 1947.

Moshe manning a Louis machine gun. Israel, 1947.

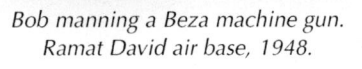

Bob manning a Beza machine gun.
Ramat David air base, 1948.

Bob in the cockpit of a C-46 Commando. Tel Nof air base, 1949.

Bob working on a B-29 at the Spartan School of Aeronautics. Tulsa, Oklahoma, 1949.

Bob (second from left) on excursion. Upper Galilee, Israel, 1951.

Bob in his Warrant Officer's uniform. Israel, 1953.

Papa and Mama. Tel Aviv, 1958.

*Shirley, Bob, and their sons Mike and Gary.
Wichita, Kansas, 1963.*

Chapter Six

A Journey by Sea

Boarding the freighter took a long time. All the passengers were herded onto the top deck, where they arranged themselves in small groups, mostly by family. We were not issued life preservers, but I didn't miss them as I had no idea that they were necessary.

Moshe and I grabbed a position at the aft of the ship next to the rail and looked forward to our first sea-voyage. Near us were some rails and planks that were rigged to hang over the edge of the ship. I did not realize that these were, in effect, outhouses. If nature called you simply stood on a plank, held on for dear life, and relieved yourself overboard. Moshe and I had to put up with a long line of people waiting for these makeshift toilets. I chalk it up to my inexperience as a sailor.

It was getting late and I fell asleep soon after boarding the ship. I was awakened by the engine noise and the sound of waves splashing against the hull. I stood up and looked over the rail. It was early morning and the ship was pulling away from the dock. It was fascinating to watch the water being churned up by the propeller. The freighter was moving briskly and rocking gently on the waves. As the ship moved out onto the Caspian Sea, the docks receded from us as if we were standing still. Gradually the city began to fade and finally all I could see was water from horizon to horizon. It felt odd to be completely out of sight of land. We were on our way. But where to?

Some said we were going to Persia, and others thought our destination would be somewhere in Africa. I had no idea what we could expect in either of those places. Thanks to my Siberian geography lessons I knew where Africa and Persia were on the map, but that was the extent of my knowledge.

Soon the waves grew larger and became capped with white foam. The ship began to sway up and down and from side to side. Some of the passengers

became seasick and vomited overboard or on deck. The sailors ordered everyone either to sit down on the deck or go below. Moshe and I did not get seasick, but many of the other children in our group did. The stench was nause-
ating. The overboard toilets were occupied all the time. We also heard rumors
that four or five people had died and the sailors had dumped the corpses overboard.

As we approached the southern end of the sea, the waves subsided and we
glided into the Persian port of Pahlevi. Before we disembarked, a search of
the ship was carried out by the Soviet border patrol. Apparently the Poles had
reported some Jewish stowaways. They were taken into custody to be shipped
back to the Soviet Union. But one of the detainees suffered a heart attack, so
the border guard decided to turn them all over to the Polish camp authorities.
The detainees were promptly claimed by the Jewish Agency, which had an office in the Pahlevi camp.

I was quite relieved when we left the ship and entered Persian territory. It
was now August of 1942, and we had been in the Soviet Union nearly two
and a half years.

From the dock we walked to a transition camp near the shores of the
Caspian Sea. Here we were introduced to showers and soap. It was the first
shower Moshe and I had ever had. In Poland Mama always bathed us in a tub.
I loved the shower in the camp, and even though the water was cold, the soap
helped take the grime off my body. For the first time in months, I felt clean
and had a pleasant odor.

Later a doctor checked us out and gave us immunization shots. From there
we walked through a large storage room and were given used but clean shirts,
pants, and shoes with socks. This was a real treat, as we had all but forgotten
what a sock looked like. Moshe and I could hardly believe our good fortune
as we ran our hands over our new outfits.

Our hostile director was gone, replaced by a general camp authority that consisted of Polish army representatives. We were led to a military-type bunk in an
open barrack with a corrugated metal roof supported by wooden posts. The dining hall served three meals a day. This splendor was unbelievable to us.

Every day was an adventure and we began to learn how to play again.
Sometimes we went for a swim in the sea or helped the local fishermen bring
in the day's catch in their nets. Yet we did not completely let down our guard.
There were other Jewish kids in the camp and we knew some of them. Even
so, Moshe and I kept our Jewish identity to ourselves. I had no idea what was
in store for us, and we behaved according to our well-honed defensive in-
stincts. It was rumored that there were quite a few Jewish children in the
camp who had become Polish Catholics by assimilation. Most of those, I suspected, had to be younger children who did not know any better.

For all practical purposes our names, as registered on the Polish exit list, were Yuzef and Mikhal. Those were common Polish names. And if it turned out that we had to go to church to survive, Moshe and I knew how to cross ourselves and recite "In the name of the Father, the Son, and the Holy Ghost, amen."

Several days had passed since our arrival in Pahlevi. Moshe and I were walking along the beach when a middle aged gentleman, wearing a light gray suit and tropical hat, approached us and struck up a conversation. "And by the way," he said, "do you know any Jewish children in camp?" I was immediately suspicious. "No, we don't," I replied. He then introduced himself as Shmuel Neeman (at least, that is my recollection), and said that he was a representative of the Jewish Agency in the Land of Israel—"Eretz Isroel," he pronounced it, with a distinct Yiddish accent. I knew that only a Jew could say these words the way he did. He also said that he was looking for Jewish children to take to the Land of Israel. When I heard this, I told him that we were Jews. He gave us a fatherly hug and said "I thought you were." I told him what our Jewish names were and we pointed out some other kids we thought were Jewish.

The Jewish Agency was quite well organized. A special area, managed by Jewish instructors, was established as a Jewish camp. Moshe and I were transferred there and were relieved not to have to play the Catholic game any longer. In the Jewish camp we found many more children our age and even younger. We were told that we would be going to the city of Tehran to await a transport to Israel, which was then under British rule and was called Palestine. When our children's group departed the camp, it filled up three buses. But I wonder how many more Jewish children never identified themselves to the Jewish Agency.

Tehran is about two hundred miles from Pahlevi and our trip followed narrow, unpaved roads through a primitive mountainous region. In retrospect I can see how dangerous it was to undertake such a journey in those old Persian buses, but we children enjoyed every minute of it. It was thrilling to make our way through mountain passes alongside sheer cliffs. And of course our strange caravan aroused the curiosity of everyone we passed.

Being on the bus with other Jewish kids gave us the chance to listen to their heartbreaking tales. Most of the children had undergone experiences similar to ours. Unfortunately many had lost at least one parent, and often both. Some of them had been separated from their parents during the war, and were taken care of by an older brother or sister who then died in the Soviet Union. There were some children who had to bury their parents in graves they dug with their own hands. Others did not know where their parents were buried. And there were some children under three years old who did not remember their parents at all. The instructors did their best to comfort and care for these little ones.

Listening to these awful stories made me feel very fortunate by comparison. One boy who was about seven years old was crying for his sister. An instructor told us that she was ill and had to be left behind in a Polish orphanage. "She will join us when she gets well," he told the boy. Four months later, a Jewish representative found her in another camp in Tehran, but she insisted that she was a Catholic and would not let the Jewish Agency claim her. Her older brother was taken over to talk to her. He confronted her in Yiddish, and that's when she broke down. More than anything, she wanted to be with her brother. The little girl said that she was given nice clothes to wear, and was told that she was a Catholic and that her parents had been Catholic. Other such children were discovered years later in Europe, and I wonder how many similar tales are still unknown to us.

After a long and bumpy ride we stopped to eat sandwiches and drink some water. Then we continued down the mountains to the plain in which Tehran lies. The road to Tehran was unpaved and rough, and the buses churned up an immense cloud of dust. Along the way we passed many poor villages and small family farms. But as we pulled into the city at dusk a bustling modern metropolis appeared before our eyes, with brightly lit shops, noisy traffic, and crowded streets.

The three buses crossed the western part of the city and came to Camp No. 1. Here we were briefed about the conditions we could expect at the camp and the regulations and timetables we would have to follow. Then we were registered and sent to another camp, about two miles away. Transition Camp No. 2, as it was called, was a large place that housed Polish refugees and army personnel who were to be trained by the British to fight in the African campaign against Rommel's Afrika Korps. This camp was evidently part of an air force base. The buildings that housed the refugees were brick structures that looked like army barracks. Several aircraft hangars had also been converted into storage and lodging facilities. The main serving kitchen was on the western edge of the camp. The camp was subdivided into sectors and it was each sector's responsibility to get the assigned portions of food and subdivide it. The records indicate that the two camps, Nos. 1 and 2, had a total population of 24,000 Polish citizens. Of these, 1,800 were Jews.[1]

At Camp No. 2 our group joined other Jewish orphans who had arrived in earlier transports. The man in charge was Mr. David Lowenberg, who looked to be in his early thirties. Mr. Lowenberg welcomed us and introduced us to the rest of the children. Many of the children asked each other questions about the whereabouts of their parents or relatives. The younger ones just stood there and didn't say anything.

The sector assigned to the Jewish orphanage was next to a runway. A brick building housed the administrative office and the children under five; the rest of the kids shared square tents, courtesy of the British army, with eight to ten children in each one. The total number of all the children in the Jewish orphanage, who later came to be known as the "Children of Tehran," came to 717—ages six months to eighteen years.[2]

One of the adult volunteers who helped at the orphanage was a man by the name of Yaacov Elyasberg, whom I remember only vaguely. Many years later I recalled him when I read the unpublished memoirs of Paul Lourie. Lourie, a Viennese plywood and veneer industrialist who managed to get out of Austria after its unification with Germany in 1938, was the grandfather of my daughter-in-law Ilana. Mr. Elyasberg, a plant manager in eastern Poland, was a relative of Lourie's.

Life at Camp No. 2 proceeded at a slow and routine pace. We exercised daily, ate well, and attended some classes. Some of the older children in the orphanage helped out with feeding and washing the younger ones, leading exercises, and so forth. Each child received two navy blue blankets—one to sleep on, and one to use as a cover at night. We were given clothing that was clean, but often ill-fitting. It was not unusual to see children in pants that were too long, shirts that were big enough to hide in or so tight that the buttons popped off, and shoes that were too large. In spite of our discomfort we were cheerful and happy. Occasionally I saw some of the girls crying silently, but as far as I was concerned our lot was not bad. It was much better than being in the Soviet Union.

Three times each day, the boys who were my age and older went to the kitchen in the Polish sector to fetch food, which we carried back in buckets to distribute to the Jewish children. To get to the kitchen it was necessary to cross the Polish Catholic sector. Most of the time we had to endure slurs, and sometimes even kicks. It was usually kids who harassed us, but occasionally adults also did so. Once in a while the Catholic children would hurl rocks in our direction and we would repay them in kind. This went on for some time until our complaints to the camp administration put a stop to it. Nevertheless, we were still on our guard when we went to the kitchen.

While at the camp in Tehran I lost track of the days and months. We were not exposed to news of any kind, so we had no idea what was going on in the world or how the war was progressing. Nor did we receive letters from our loved ones. Fortunately, however, our adult caretakers told us when the high holidays of Rosh Hashana and Yom Kippur were at hand.

When Rosh Hashana approached a delegation of Jews from Tehran invited some of us to partake in the festivals. A group of children were also selected to stay in Jewish homes for the holidays. It came as a surprise when on Yom

Kippur the Mizrahi (Middle Eastern) Jews of Persia came to pick up the children in their cars. Among the Ashkenazi Jews of Eastern Europe, driving a car or doing any other kind of work was strictly forbidden on the Sabbath, and Yom Kippur was considered the Sabbath of Sabbaths. In addition, we were surprised to learn that the Mizrahi Jews pronounced Hebrew in an unfamiliar manner. The Mizrahi Hebrew is authentic, whereas the Ashkenazi is somewhat distorted. The Mizrahi hymns also had different tunes, and some of the rituals were unfamiliar as well. Other than these differences, the holidays felt unmistakably Jewish.

The storeroom in the main building contained, among other things, big stacks of men's suits. None of us children wore suits, and I don't recall any of the adults wearing them either. More than once, Moshe and I and some of the other kids sneaked into the storage compartment, which was separated from the younger children's sleeping quarters by a curtain of blankets that had been pinned together. Each one of us put on two or more suits and walked out to the gate to sell them to the Persians who hung out there looking for a chance to make a *tuman*, which was what their currency was called. I conducted the transactions in sign language and was able to sell a number of suits this way. I do not recall when and why we stopped selling them. I imagine the storeroom ran out of inventory. I also don't remember how much money we made from those sales, and no doubt we were cheated. But at least we had money to buy some fruit.

I had never seen a pomegranate before we came to Tehran. The first time I ate one, I struggled to open it and to eat the multitude of red seeds inside, which I found to be somewhat bitter. Seeing me fighting to get at the fruit and spitting out the seeds, one of the vendors showed me how to eat it. You squeeze the pomegranate all around until the seeds release the juice. When the fruit feels soft and liquid inside, you punch a pinhole in the skin and suck out the sweet juice and discard the rest. After I learned how to eat them, pomegranates became my favorite fruit.

I never owned a wrist-watch, but the money I made from selling the suits made it possible for me to buy one. I found a vendor who had watches hanging from his belt, so I picked out one and paid for it. Moshe also bought one, but lost it later on. I really did not notice whether the watch kept correct time, but I felt important just wearing a wrist-watch. We also spent some of the money on candy.

Around September or October, I succumbed to an infectious skin disease that was going around the camp. Moshe did not get it, but many of the other children did. The disease was very contagious and everyone who came down with it was quarantined. Its first symptom was the appearance of blisters between the fingers that were filled with yellow liquid and itched terribly. It was very similar to poison ivy. Then it spread all over the body from head to toe. We were quarantined in a large military tent. Moshe came to visit me and we talked across the fence. After about three days, the itching subsided and the blisters dried up.

Several days after I was released from quarantine, I had another bout with malaria. This time it was not too bad because I was given quinine, and in a few days I was better.

As time passed, many of our Polish friends were shipped out to various destinations, but our group seemed to linger longer than anyone else. Years later I read in a report regarding the Children of Tehran that a diplomatic effort had been made in Britain to arrange for us to fly to Palestine via Iraq. But the state of Iraq refused to let us fly over their air space. Another option was to take us by bus through Turkey and then by ship to Palestine. That kind of trip, however, was full of dangers: the roads were bad and in some cases nonexistent, there were rumors of bandits controlling certain areas, and our buses were not in very good shape. Going through Turkey would also have entailed traveling through territory with no medical facilities. So the diplomatic haggling dragged on. Britain also had to make a special exception for us, because our numbers exceeded the immigration quota to Palestine. To appease the Arabs Britain had established minimal quotas for Jewish immigrants. All of these problems delayed our departure.

It was now November, and it began to snow. The nights were freezing and the tents were unheated. The adults were very concerned about what would happen to the children when winter arrived in full force. Meanwhile, we children improvised ways to stay warm. We had no cots, so we slept on blankets spread out on the ground. To keep warm at night, all the children in a tent would sleep together, using some of their blankets for a ground cover and piling the rest on top of them. You stayed warm this way unless you happened to be on the edge, and then you had to tug on the covers all night long. During the day, we would wrap the blankets around our shoulders for extra protection against the cold.

In late December of 1942, we were told to pack and get ready to leave for the Land of Israel. What little I knew about Eretz Israel came from stories I had heard when I was growing up in Poland. Our house had a charity box on the wall with a picture of Jerusalem on it, and my mother used to put in some coins whenever she had any to spare—"to help Eretz Isroel," she said. But the rabbis at the religious school or *cheder* I attended in Chelm never made any connection between Eretz Israel and the Hebrew scriptures. I rather doubt that any of those rabbis could have pointed out Palestine on a map. And when we recited prayers that mentioned Yerushalayim, I somehow did not associate this city with the place where my mother was sending her coins. Perhaps this was because all the biblical stories seemed like fairy tales and legends to me. So when the Polish Catholics used to scream *Zhydy do Palestyny!* ("Jews to Palestine!"), I had no idea what they were talking about.

It was only in Tehran that I was exposed to the history of the Jews, and finally was able to relate the scriptures to the land whose name I had heard so often. I felt like a thick curtain had been raised and now I could see clearly. The teachers told us about the pioneers that settled Eretz Israel, and how the land was being revived from the neglect of two thousand years of desolation. I felt proud of my heritage. Now, I thought, I would have a country of my own and would have no further need of the Polacks. I was going home, where my forefathers Avraham, Yitzhak, and Yaacov had lived and were laid to rest.

The train transported us to the port of Khorramshahr, located on a river near Abadan on the Persian Gulf. We boarded a freighter called the *Doniera* to take us to Karachi in what was then part of the British colony of India, but is now Pakistan. Before boarding the ship one of the boys, David Tzvibl, collected money in the form of Persian tuman from some of the other boys and exchanged it for U.S. dollars. I exchanged some of my money in this way and spent all of it on candy.

The freighter was part of a military troop transport. We occupied the aft end of the ship and settled down on the floor of the lower deck. The front was taken up by African soldiers and soldiers from New Zealand in British uniforms.

When the ship set out, it maneuvered around so that it would be heading south towards the gulf. As the ship turned, its huge propellers churned up the muddy waters of the river. I watched the color of the water change gradually from brown to light green, dark green, and finally to blue as the ship entered the Persian Gulf. Once in the gulf, the freighter steamed along over a smooth sea. To the right, the shoreline of the Arabian Peninsula was distinctly visible, while to the left the outline of the Persian coast was shrouded in a veil of haze.

As we neared the Straight of Hormuz off the coast of Oman, the shores on both sides seemed to close in on us. Before long we had passed through the straight and into the Gulf of Oman, the gateway to the Arabian Sea.

The soldiers on the ship were friendly, especially those from New Zealand. They tried to teach us to say English words and gave us chocolates and sweet biscuits. The sea was calm, and I do not recall anyone getting seasick. All the while, sailors scanned the horizon with binoculars. They were searching for German submarines. One of the sailors let me have a look for myself. I had never held binoculars before, and I was amazed at how close the horizon seemed to be. I wanted to keep looking through the binoculars, but the sailor had to have them back.

The ship was also equipped with a small-caliber cannon which the crew used to shoot at empty cartons for practice. We also practiced the "abandon ship "routine, and learned how to put on life vests when the siren sounded.

When we were about a day out, we encountered a small convoy that included steamers and British navy frigates, all heading east. One frigate came up close to our ship and the sailors waved at us. I was surprised to see how small the naval ship seemed next to our freighter. But the frigate had many cannons and machine guns.

At one point our crew lowered two torpedo-shaped devices into the water. These were attached to cables and dragged behind the ship. I was told that this was some sort of sonar. All of these activities were very entertaining and kept me on the top deck most of the time. I tried once to go down to see what the engine room was like, but I was stopped by a sailor.

By now our constant companion of hunger—so much a part of our lives in the U.S.S.R.—had disappeared, and so had my scheming to obtain food. Sometimes, when I was topside alone at night, I stretched out on the deck under the black, star-studded sky and felt very small. Then my thoughts would drift back to my parents. I longed for the comfort of my mother and her smiling blue eyes. I recalled the times she spent standing in line for hours to get bread for Moshe and me, and her endless quest to find medicine when I was sick. I felt quite alone in that vast wilderness of sky and sea. What was I going to do, I wondered, when we got to the Land of Israel? Where would I live, and how would I support my twelve-year-old brother? Who was going to hire a boy of fifteen? And what about school? All these unanswerable questions were stuck in my mind as in a spider web.

I lost track of time and do not recall how many days we were at sea. But after maybe three or four days, we eased into the port of Karachi. It was now around the beginning of January, 1943.

The port of Karachi was bristling with huge cranes on rail tracks, loading and unloading hundreds of ships packed with what seemed to be military equipment. There were also many beggars sleeping on the pavement near the docks. Those poor people had only loincloths covering their bodies and seemed to be starving.

We left the freighter holding hands in groups of two, and proceeded to an army truck that would take us to our destination in a British transit camp. On our way to the camp we drove through the city. Karachi looked dirty and chaotic. People were milling about everywhere. Most of the people were barefoot and had very little clothing on their bodies. Luckily it was hot in the daytime.

Soon we passed a construction site where large elephants were being put to work. The elephants were pulling logs and carrying loads with their trunks while being directed by a man who was perched on the head of one of them. The children watched in amazement. I had never seen an elephant at work, although I had once seen an elephant in a circus that came to Chelm when I was about seven years old.

After traveling a short distance we arrived at a British Army camp situated in a desolate plain. There were a few British officers and soldiers in the camp, but otherwise it was practically empty. The entire camp consisted of three or four wooden barracks and a flagpole flying the Union Jack. There were also several military tents like the ones we had in Tehran that had apparently been set up in preparation for our arrival. Here, however, the tents were arranged end-to-end with open flaps so as to form one long structure that could house all the children together. Both walls of this big tent were lined with army cots. We were issued pith helmets just like some of the British soldiers wore to shade us from the harsh sun. Our blankets were to be used for padding the cots. It was the first time in months that I did not have to sleep on the ground or a floor.

To our pleasure and surprise, the camp had an outdoor movie theater. This was a first for us, as Moshe and I had no idea that there even was such a thing as an outdoor movie theater. We never missed a show. For additional entertainment, I pulled up a bamboo stick that was propping up the tent wall and used it to fashion a bow and arrow set. I tried out my arrows on a flock of vultures that scavenged at a dump on the outskirts of the camp, but the big birds outsmarted me. Those vultures seemed to be able to judge the distance my arrows could fly, and always stayed a few yards out of range. I finally gave up on the vultures and settled for target practice.

Among the children was a teenager about my age by the name of Avraham Goldman (no relation) who had been born in Warsaw. The boy was a very gifted artist. With great ease, he could sketch a likeness of a person in just a few minutes. As a token of his appreciation for the hospitality extended to us by the British, Avraham sculpted a white Polish eagle, the emblem of Poland, with an inscription that read: "Thank you for the hospitality, from the Citizens of Poland." The emblem was presented to the British base commander, who put the sculpture on a pedestal at the foot of the flagpole.

The camp commander organized a trip to the city zoo. Only a few children were selected to go, and I was one of the lucky ones. But Moshe, who was not chosen, was heartbroken, so I traded places with him. The trip took all day and the kids had much fun. Moshe later described to me all the different animals he had seen. He was very excited, and I was happy that he had had such a good time.

The days in Karachi flew by. After three weeks, we were told to get ready to move out. It didn't take us long. We had only to roll up our blankets and put on our new pith helmets, and we were all set. Once again, we were loaded into army trucks and driven to the port, where we were to board a troop transport. This ship was called the *Neoralia*. It was bigger than the *Doniera* and the food was better. But there were more troops on board and the discipline was stricter.

All of us children were put below the first deck in the aft part of the ship, and we were ordered to stay in our assigned area except to visit the deck. I went up and watched while a big cannon was loaded onto the ship and mounted on a special platform.

We all received hammocks to sleep in. We enjoyed sleeping or resting in these hammocks, and at times we would use them as swings. We also pulled pranks by loosening the rope at one end of a hammock so that it would collapse when someone tried to get in it. Our instructors didn't think this was funny, however, and they made us stop.

We went to sleep while the ship was still in port. The next morning I awoke to a gentle rocking. I jumped up and ran upstairs. We were at sea, and we were not alone. In fact, we were part of an armada that stretched as far as the eye could see. There were British cruisers, huge battle ships with the biggest guns I had ever seen, and many cargo ships and troop transports like ours. The ships were also signaling to each other. It was a thrilling sight.

The next day our ship participated in naval exercises. The ship did some zig-zagging and the sailors fired the big cannon several times. Shortly after that, our ship broke away from the armada and sailed toward the Red Sea.

As we neared the Red Sea, the crew was constantly on the lookout for German submarines. As I look back, I realize that we children had no idea of the danger we faced as passengers on a troop transport. To us, the whole thing was just another adventure.

Soon we arrived in the port of Aden, the capital of Yemen. The port is situated near the entrance to the Red Sea, at the base of a towering range of black, arid mountains on the southern tip of the Arabian Peninsula. The ship anchored a short distance from the city to unload some cargo. From our position the port looked dirty, with a gloomy and treeless city behind it.

As soon as we dropped anchor, barges full of half-naked Yemenites pulled up to our ship's portside to unload bags of coal. They formed a human chain from their barges to the ship's hold, and they unloaded the coal by passing the bags from one man to the next. The Yemenites shouted and gestured the whole time. Someone threw some coins in the water and several Yemenites dived for them. Sometimes two men came up fighting for the same coin. We tossed some bread down and they dove for that as well. Once or twice the sailors had to fire warning shots into the water to keep a Yemenite from climbing up one of the ship's ropes.

When the loading job was done, our ship pulled up anchor and sailed into the Red Sea. We entered the Gulf of Suez a few days later. On the starboard side lay the Sinai Peninsula—the very same Sinai that Moses crossed during the Exodus from Egypt. Somehow I had visualized the Sinai rather differently when I studied the Bible. My child's mind couldn't imagine the heat and emptiness of the desert.

Our ship glided slowly into the port of Suez at the southern end of the Suez Canal. This was where we were to disembark. Our arrival was anticipated by soldiers serving in the Jewish Brigade of the British Army. These men in uniform simply could not do enough for us. They took care of us as if we were their own flesh and blood. Many of the soldiers had relatives in the areas of Poland from which we came, and some even found relatives among the children. We were showered with candy and questions. After refreshments, we were divided into groups to board a train to Palestine.

The view from the train, which ran parallel to the Suez canal, was interesting. The ships sailing through the canal looked like big boats in a river moving along very slowly. Here and there we could see anti-aircraft batteries manned by British soldiers.

Eventually the train turned east to continue along the shore of the Mediterranean Sea. The first station we came to was the Arab city of Gaza in southern Palestine. It was here that I first saw the traditional Arab garb. The men wore ankle-long robes and scarves with ropes tied around them to keep them in place. Some of the Arabs were barefoot and some wore sandals. The whole atmosphere of the station was depressing. The dirty-looking colonial policemen and the goats and sheep that were present reminded me of Uzbekistan.

Soon we reached the first Jewish farms and the land became green. When we saw the little white farm cottages surrounded by lush vegetation we were suddenly overtaken with joy. The symmetry of the fields and the beauty of the gardens with their irrigating sprinklers was a sight I will never forget. It was the first time in my life I had seen sprinklers at work, and I was fascinated by this artificial rain. Some of the passengers on the train burst out with the song Hevenu Shalom Aleichem, "We're Bringing Peace to You." Even though I didn't understand the words, it sounded very happy.

Our eyes were glued to the train windows as we passed farm after farm. We waved and our countrymen waved back at us. It felt good to see Jewish farmers. All the farmers I had ever known were Poles and Soviets. Historically, Jews were not allowed to own land, so they strayed away from their tradition of farming. But here the Jews had taken up where they left off.

Our next stop was the Jewish city of Rehovot. What a contrast to Gaza! This was a pretty town with nice streets, orderly traffic, and neatly-dressed people. Words cannot describe the elation in our hearts when we pulled into the station. Men, women, and children rushed into the cars, bearing gifts of food and boxes full of oranges—for it was the season when oranges were harvested.

Up to that point in my life, I had eaten exactly one half of an orange. I was eight years old at the time. I recall our family going for a stroll one Saturday afternoon in the summer. We walked by a fruit stand and I pointed to the oranges and asked my parents what they were. They stopped to tell us about how oranges grow in Eretz Israel. Although oranges were very expensive in Poland, my father bought one and split it between Moshe and me. I never forgot the delicious taste of that fruit. And here we were, being showered with oranges.

We grabbed all of the fruit we could hold on to. We ate and ate until we could eat no more. The people watched us in disbelief. They had tears in their eyes.

I was still on the defensive, not being able yet to get used to the idea that here we were all Jews, that Hebrew was the national language, and that I would never have to fight just because of who I was. It was only gradually that I acquired the feeling of belonging, the sense that these were truly my people, and that the pieces to the puzzle of my life were beginning to fall into place.

After the joyous reception our train was ready to leave. As we pulled away from Rehovot, the crowd burst out with the song Hatikvah, which would later become the national anthem of Israel. So now Hatikvah would also be my anthem. A warm feeling that I had never experienced before went through me—a feeling of pride in my ancestry.

The train continued north, passing by many Jewish farms and through many towns. It continued along the Mediterranean Sea until we came to Atlit, a British transit camp south of Haifa. Here we disembarked.

Atlit was a prisoner-of-war camp that the British had converted into a transit camp for processing new immigrants to Palestine. It was a typical camp with barbed wire and barracks and the inevitable watchtowers, but it was free of guards, and you could come and go as you pleased. I noted the date and burned it into my mind—February 10, 1943. The day I came home.

NOTES

1. Greenberg, *Children of Zion*, 17–18.
2. Greenberg, *Children of Zion*, 218.

Chapter Seven

I Become a Sabra

Atlit was a flurry of activity. Doctors gave us physical examinations and we were fitted with new clothes. Men and women also came to the camp to interview us. They asked where we were from and what we had experienced, and they wanted to know about relatives and Jewish friends that we might have left behind in the U.S.S.R. Some time later, I got a letter from my parents thanking me for sending them food and clothing. Evidently the Jewish Agency had arranged for care packages to be sent to the people whose names and addresses we had provided.

One of those who interviewed us was the famous Henrietta Szold, the founder of Hadassah and creator of the Youth Aliyah program that saved tens of thousands of Jewish children from the Nazis by making it possible for them to immigrate to Palestine. She was unknown to me then, but a year later my school visited Jerusalem and we went to see her in the offices of the Youth Aliyah. Ms. Szold talked to us about education, life in Eretz Israel, and so forth. At one point, she asked me my name, and when I told her she said "And how is your brother Moshe?" I was astonished. This great and dedicated lady—who never took time to start a family of her own—regarded the young refugees as her children, and like any mother she never forgot any of us.

After all of the examinations and interviews, some of which involved psychological evaluation, Moshe and I were adopted by a religious labor party called Hapoel Hamizrakhi ("The Eastern Worker"). Together with seventy other children between the ages of thirteen and seventeen, we were sent to the boarding school Mikveh Israel, which means "Israel's Hope." Mikveh Israel, established in 1880, was located south of Tel Aviv and was the most famous agronomy school in the country. This was to be my home for the next two years.

Mikveh Israel had two educational programs, one secular (the "State School") and the other religious (the "State Religious School"). Apparently the interviewers in Atlit had decided that we came from a traditional family, so Moshe and I were enrolled in the latter. Had I known of this decision I would probably have objected. In any case, the boys and girls were divided into three groups, ranging from oldest to youngest. I was in the second group, which was called "Bet," and Moshe in the third, called "Gimel"—aleph, bet, and gimel being the first three letters of the Hebrew alphabet.

My group was assigned to a two-story brick and stucco building near a eucalyptus grove. The girls were housed upstairs and the boys downstairs, with six or seven children to a room. We were each given a steel-framed bed with a mattress, two sheets, and a blanket and pillow. We were also assigned private lockers. Each week we received clean sheets and a change of clothes, stamped with our names and classes for identification, and our dirty clothes and sheets were taken to a collective laundry to be washed. We ate three good meals a day in the common dining-room.

The whole point of our education at Mikveh Israel was to mold us into productive citizens of a future Jewish state. We studied four hours a day, and the rest of the time we worked. Our work involved learning the various branches of agriculture so that we could understand how farms function. We spent one month in each branch. Our academic studies focused on Hebrew language and Jewish history, although we also learned mathematics, chemistry, and other subjects related to agriculture. Since Moshe and I were in the religious school, we studied biblical history from a religious point of view. The students in the secular school, on the other hand, studied the Bible strictly as a history of the Jewish people.

As I learned Hebrew, I began to appreciate the Hebrew Bible more and more. I came to understand the connections between the Jewish traditions of my childhood and the history of my people. This made me feel proud to be a Jew, and I began to think that, instead of embracing anti-Semitism, the Christians should be thankful to us for the gift of our Torah. My increasing knowledge of the land and language of Eretz Israel also made me start to feel like a native Israeli or "Sabra." (The name comes from fruit of a certain cactus, which is prickly on the outside and sweet on the inside.)

The State School students came from various kibbutzim (communal farms) and moshavim (private farms), and most were not at all religious. In the Religious School, however, we lived the life of observant Jews. We had to pray three times a day, to observe all Jewish holidays, and to keep the Sabbath in accordance with religious tradition. Some of our customs were heartwarming, such as singing Biblical hymns after meals. The traditional prayers also brought back fond memories from my childhood.

After a while I learned how to recite the prayers by heart. What is more, my new knowledge of Hebrew made it possible for me to understand their meaning and to appreciate the poetry of the Bible. As time passed, however, I began to question both the Jewish faith and religion in general. It seemed to me that religion was a source of animosity among human beings. I also thought that many religious laws and customs had become antiquated and needed to be changed—an idea that was strongly opposed by those who believed these laws were given by God. I had frequent disputes on this subject with my religious teacher, who was a Hasidic Jew. But although I was drifting toward secularism, I still had a sentimental attachment to our religious tradition.

Mikveh Israel was under the jurisdiction of a Jewish Settlement Police constable. The constable was a British appointee, as were all members of the Settlement Police, and had custody of a dozen Royal Enfield rifles for defense purposes. The school was also guarded by an Arab who lived with his family in a small house by the main gate.

An important part of our integration into Israeli society was learning how to defend ourselves from enemies. After we had been at Mikveh Israel for about six months, it was time for us to become part of the Jewish Defense Force—the Haganah. The Haganah was, however, an illegal organization, having been outlawed by the British Mandate (the colonial government of Palestine). In fact, any Jew caught with firearms risked being sentenced to death by hanging. The process of enlistment therefore had to be carried out on an individual basis and in strict secrecy.

One night, I was ordered to go to a shed in an orange grove. When I approached the shed, a man came out from behind a tree and asked me who I was and where I was going. He seemed satisfied with my answers and directed me to a small cottage nearby. When I walked in, I was shocked to see our police constable sitting at a desk along with several other men. On the desk there was a Bible and a semiautomatic Mauser pistol. I was asked if I wanted to join the Haganah. Without hesitation, I said yes. I was sworn in, holding the Bible in one hand and the gun in the other. With tears in my eyes, I took an oath to defend my country, my heritage, and my freedom. I was also sworn to uphold the secrecy of the Haganah. I was sixteen years old.

After my initiation into the Haganah—a process that all of the students at Mikveh Israel went through—I began training in warfare and self-defense. We learned to climb trees and to use ropes to cross from tree to tree. We learned K.A.P.A.P., a kind of hand-to-hand combat that involved clubs. We would stand in a circle and our trainer would attack us at random, aiming blows to the head, chin, knees, and other parts of the body. Our goal was to keep from getting hit. Once in a while we did get hit, but generally the results were not serious.

The next phase of training involved handguns. We learned to assemble, disassemble, and clean several types of pistols, including Berettas, Mausers, Parabellums, and revolvers. We also trained with the rifles in the constable's office. During this part of the training we posted guards to watch for British patrols. When a patrol approached, we took our equipment to a previously determined hideaway.

Our school also arranged hikes that were designed to familiarize us with the topography and geography of the country and to allow us to see how various kibbutzim operated their farms. The deeper purpose of these hikes was to help us prepare to function as soldiers. While on the kibbutzim we trained with arms and visited the nearby Arab villages. We wanted to learn all that we could about the Arabs. Most of the Arab villages benefited from their proximity to the Jewish farms, which often employed them and sometimes gave them medical and technical assistance. This suggested to me that Jews and Arabs could coexist peacefully.

The first kibbutz we hiked to was Tirat Zvi in the Bet Shean valley. This valley lies south of Lake Kinneret, which is better known outside Israel as the Sea of Galilee. Tirat Zvi was truly a pioneering kibbutz. It still had a stockade surrounding it, complete with a watchtower. It was part of a defensive chain of settlements along with the nearby kibbutzim of Yad Elyahu and Maoz Khaim. In the event of an Arab attack the residents of these kibbutzim would rally to help one another. At such times the farmers communicated by short-wave radio or by Morse code sent from the towers.

The climate at the kibbutz was quite harsh, with temperatures reaching 110 to 120 degrees Fahrenheit in the sun. I was assigned to irrigation duty. Most of the fields were irrigated with water from Artesian wells. After I opened the water gate to the irrigation ditch, I would jump into the spouting well to keep cool until the ditch filled up. I also carried a clay jug with drinking water in it, which was cooled by the evaporation of water absorbed by the clay.

At Tirat Zvi we continued our training with clubs. This time our trainer was a member of the kibbutz, who was very good at his job. To demonstrate his skill he would put a cigarette in someone's mouth and knock it out with one swing of his club. This same instructor also introduced us to a new weapon: the King David rock sling. This was a simple but dangerous device. The sling was made of two four-foot lengths of rope and a small flexible leader. You looped one end of the rope around your little finger and held the other end in the same hand. A fist-sized rock was placed in the leader and then you swung the sling around. When the sling got up speed, you opened up your hand and the rock flew out. This weapon could easily kill or disable a person. During one of the training sessions, in fact, a flying rock was deflected by a wall and struck one of our boys in his left eye. He was rushed to the clinic but his eye could not be saved.

When we got back from Tirat Zvi we continued with our studies. It was now 1944. Details of the Holocaust had begun to come out. We received information about the German murder of entire Jewish communities, including that of Chelm, the city of my birth. Several of my older classmates left school and signed up to join the Jewish Brigade of the British Army. Their aim was to fight the Germans in order to avenge their loved ones. I also wanted to join the Brigade. I went with a couple of friends to Tel Aviv to sign up, but the recruiter told us to return when we were eighteen.

I had reached the point in my studies when it was time to choose a major subject. I had an aptitude for technical work, so I decided to concentrate on agricultural machinery. I felt that this would build on my training in the Soviet Union. My instructor was David Leibowitz, a likeable man with whom I hit it off from the start. He had emigrated from Russia, so we had something in common. We had classes in the morning, and in the afternoon we worked in the tractor garage. I learned a few things about Caterpillar tractors, and I also learned how to repair electric irons and sewing machines.

I was very proud of one accomplishment in particular—a slide projector that I constructed from old flashlight lenses. I built a sheet-metal housing for the lenses, although in doing so I managed to cut my right index finger quite badly. Then I mounted the lenses on a movable base that would allow me to adjust the focus. Next I built a reflector for a light bulb and mounted it behind the lenses. I rigged up two thread-spools with cranks and put them between the lens and the reflector. I used transparent paper that I got from the kitchen to draw caricatures of some of the students and teachers. The director of the religious school was impressed with my project and invited the entire school for a slide-show. It was a success, and the director congratulated me in public.

I was very lucky to have David Leibowitz as my instructor, as he was a fine inventor. When the War of Independence began in 1948 he designed a mortar that became known as the "David'ka," so named in honor of David Ben-Gurion, Israel's first Prime Minister. We Israelis had very few heavy arms, including mortars and cannons, so David used a metal gas bottle from a welding rig to fashion a mortar. He cut off one end of the bottle and mounted it on a steel platform. Then he adapted a fire extinguisher to use as the explosive shell. His contraption worked most of the time. I say "most of the time" because the shell occasionally exploded inside the tube. To be safe, I was told, the shell had to be dropped into the tube with the aid of a device that allowed the operator to stand a safe distance away. But when the David'ka *did* work, the incoming shell made an awful noise, and the powerful explosion that followed sounded like a nuclear weapon. In fact, during the war some of our spies once infiltrated the largely Arab city of Tzfat in the Galilee and spread the word that the Jews were getting ready to attack with an atomic bomb. The

David'ka was then used once, after which the entire Arab population of the city fled.

I was now at an age when girls were very interesting to me. I had my share of puppy-love flings, but none of them lasted long.

A new group of children arrived from Turkey, and I was assigned to lead their bus to the building where they would be housed. The boys and girls were quite different from the rest of us. They were Sephardic Jews and spoke Ladino as well as French. The girls were dressed nicely and wore heavy nets over their long hair. These new arrivals were set up in their own separate classes. The rest of us simply called them "the Turks."

Our group continued to hike around the country as part of our military training. One of our trips took us to Kibbutz Ein Gev on the eastern shore of Lake Kinneret. We visited the entire Galilee region and climbed the tallest mountain in the area, Mount Germack. Ein Gev is situated at the base of Mount Susita and is part of the Golan Heights. On top of Susita there was a Syrian outpost. Our training exercise was to climb up to the outpost and back without being detected by the Syrians. I enjoyed the excitement of this adventure. Luckily for us, everything came off without a hitch.

Back in school we were considered seniors, and some of my classmates were recruited into Haganah Memkaff courses, which would train them to become second lieutenants. I wanted to enter this program, but our director was looking for older candidates. So I had to remain content with continuing my training in the sands of Holon, which lay to the southeast of our school. One dark night we had a regional meeting and group swearing-in ceremony. We held torches and listened to speeches by Haganah commanders while standing in a depression between some sand dunes so that the British would not catch us.

Some of the arms we used in our training were made under the noses of the British police. One of them was a copy of the British Sten gun. Parts were made in different machine shops and brought together for assembly in various Haganah hideouts, called "sliks." We also manufactured hand grenades with four-second friction fuses. On the casting of the grenades we stamped the letters "USA." The British could not figure out what this signified, but it stood for a Yiddish phrase meaning "our self-made work" (*unsere selbständige Arbeit*). When the British did find an arms cache, they would confiscate the weapons and sometimes turn them over to the Arabs.

It was the beginning of 1945, and we students in the "Bet" group at Mikveh Israel had one more hike to make before graduation. The first part of our trip consisted of a bus ride to Jerusalem, where we went on a brief tour. It was an emotional experience for me to encounter the history of our people in the stones and monuments of the Old City and the Western Wall. To this day, my eyes mist up when I read the sign one sees when entering the city from Tel Aviv, "Pray for the Peace of Yerushalayim." From Jerusalem we took an Arab-owned bus to Bethlehem. The bus dropped us off at the Tomb of Rachel, the wife of the patriarch Jacob. The tomb looked just like it did on the postage stamps.

From Bethlehem we hiked up into the mountains to the kibbutz of Kfar Etzion in the region called Gush Etzion. The kibbutz lies above the Pools of King Solomon in the valley below. At the time this kibbutz was new, having just been settled two years earlier. Its population consisted of about three dozen dedicated couples. They greeted us warmly and treated us to a nice meal.

The kibbutz was strategically located on a mountain that overlooked a wide area. To the east one could see the Dead Sea, and to the west, if it was a clear day, the Mediterranean. Opposite the kibbutz, on a mountain above the Pools of Solomon, there was a Russian Orthodox church—a sturdy structure made from massive rocks that had been quarried nearby.

There was a chronic shortage of water in Gush Etzion. The kibbutz collected rainfall in underground cisterns, but not enough to suffice for all its needs. In order to irrigate their land, the kibbutz had to recycle sewage water. The long-term plan was to dam up a triangle of mountains to create an artificial lake that would be about two hundred feet deep. This would give the entire region plenty of water for irrigation and other uses.

We had been brought to Kfar Etzion to work. Our task was to clear boulders from the mountainside and construct terraces for a vineyard and an orchard. The work was hard, but we were young and full of energy. We tackled the rocks with a vengeance and made good progress. The soil was rich, and after we had broken rocks and made them into a retaining wall, we cleared the land and leveled it for planting. I received much satisfaction from this labor, because it contributed directly to the welfare of the kibbutz as a whole and made me feel like I was an important part of its communal life.

Kfar Etzion was a religious kibbutz, so we had to get up in the morning to pray. We also had to pray in the afternoon and evening, and before and after meals. I used to rush though the prayers, but I liked the familiar songs that we sang in the evening.

After a day's work we would wash up and have dinner in the dining hall, which was in a solid stone building that also housed the offices of the kibbutz. (The only other structures at Kfar Etzion were temporary barracks.) Meat was scarce, but there was plenty of other food, including fruit, vegetables, and bread. No one left the table hungry.

One cool evening I walked out of the dining hall after dinner and sat under a huge fig tree looking off toward the west. The setting was serene and I felt relaxed. I let my mind wander back over the history of the land and of the Jewish people. What would it have been like, I wondered, if I had the power to correct the mistakes of our Kings and Judges? What would have happened had Israel remained united with Judea? Or had the Zealots not taken over Jerusalem? Or had Shaul from Tarsus, better known as Paul, not gone to preach to the gentiles? In my mind's eye I could see a people growing strong and flourishing, a people who had never left the land I was now working so hard to reclaim, and whose roots in this land were four thousand years old. But all of this was just a daydream.

Our time at Kfar Etzion was soon up, and we prepared to return to school. We decided that we would hike back to Mikveh Israel. We went directly west toward the Mediterranean, descending single-file from the hills of Judea into the fertile plains. We passed many farms and villages, and reached home hungry and dirty after a long, hard march. The first thing I did was to jump into the irrigation pool to cool off. Then I took a shower and went to the dining hall to feast on vegetables and fresh bread.

My senior classmates, the ones in Group Aleph, were graduating. Most of the young men and women in that group decided to start a kibbutz of their own. In order to do so they would need some training, and they arranged to receive their Hakhshara or "Preparation" at Kfar Etzion. Many of the seniors had already paired up with a view to marriage, and their graduation party was a joyous event at which the dancing continued late into the night.

I was to graduate three months after Group Aleph and join them at Kfar Etzion along with the rest of Group Bet. I had already decided, however, that I was not going to continue my association with the religious movement. I debated whether to move to a city or to join a secular kibbutz. I particularly liked Ashdot Ya'acov and Afikim, kibbutzim that were located in the Jordan Valley. But I made no decision, figuring that I could do so when Moshe's class graduated some six months hence.

Luckily enough, a distant relative of my roommate Moshe Butman offered him a job in his small lock-making factory in Tel Aviv. I asked Butman if his relative could also accommodate me. He was able to do so, and after graduation we set out for Tel Aviv. We had no money, and virtually our only possessions were the clothes on our backs. It was 1945, and I was seventeen years old.

Avrom Frosh and his family had a cottage on the outskirts of north Tel Aviv near the Yarkon River. The cottage had a little garden and a small lawn in front. Butman and I were to stay with Mr. Frosh and his two very young daughters until we could find a place of our own. We slept on the floor in the dining room and worked in Mr. Frosh's factory as machinists. For this we received room and board and a little money. To us, however, it was exciting to be living in the big city of Tel Aviv. Butman and I went for strolls on the beach and watched the pretty girls. We enjoyed this even though we didn't have enough money to ask anyone out to a movie.

Mr. Frosh's factory had a lathe and a drill press and not much else. One day I was working on the lathe and I reached up to pull down the overhead light so I could see better. The next thing I knew, I was on the floor on the other side of the shop. I found that I had pulled the entire electric cord out of the ceiling. Evidently the ceramic socket with the light bulb in it was chipped, and as I reached up to pull the light closer I made contact with the exposed socket while my other hand rested on the metal lathe. This created a perfect circuit for 220 volts of electricity to pass through my body. I was lucky to be alive. In those days there were no regulations governing employee safety. If there had been, Mr. Frosh's shop, along with many others, would have been out of business.

A month after my accident, Butman and I were laid off. Mr. Frosh explained that there weren't enough orders for locks. At the same time as we lost our jobs, we also lost our room and board.

Butman and I soon found another place to live. We rented a room from a man named Braginsky on Zhabotinsky Street. At one time this area was on the outskirts of Tel Aviv, but today it is practically in the center of the city. Mr. Braginsky was a Russian who had emigrated to Palestine after the communist revolution. He worked in the Dubek cigarette factory and needed the rent income to help him finish building his house, which he was constructing from cement blocks. The house consisted of two small rooms separated by a kitchen, shower room, and toilet. Braginsky and his wife and daughter lived in one room, and Butman and I, along with two fellows named Moshe Olek and Asher Halpern—former classmates from Mikveh Israel—shared the other. Adjacent to our window was a tin shack, about ten feet square, that housed an Arab man along with his wife, children, goats, and chickens.

Every Saturday my roommates and I slept late. When we got up we would buy eggs and vegetables from the Arab and bread and wine in the nearby grocery store. We would then pitch in to make six scrambled eggs and a huge salad, and would eat this along with half a loaf of bread and wine for each of us. After that we would go to the beach, meet friends, and buy tickets to the movies. We ate our evening meal in a worker's cafeteria. The food was cheap, but it nearly always gave us indigestion.

I was able to pay for all of this because I had found a job in another factory that also manufactured locks, among other things. This factory had a nice tool and dye department. The tool and dye maker sometimes let me assist him. He showed me how to do various sorts of precision work, including making a perfectly straight steel block with a hand file. My Haganah commander, Dov, worked in the same factory operating an automatic nail machine. Although Dov was called away for various duties by the Haganah, he never discussed them with me.

It was now the autumn of 1945. The war in Europe was over, and the United States had used the atomic bomb to put an end to Japanese aggression. But for us, a new war was just beginning. The British were reneging on the Balfour Declaration's promise of a Jewish state in Palestine, and had announced continued restrictions on Jewish immigration.

My brother Moshe's class was graduating, and I went down to Mikveh Israel for the occasion. His class, Group Gimel, had decided to go south in preparation for founding a new kibbutz. Moshe and I discussed his prospects, and I advised him to pursue welding. After their graduation Group Gimel went to Moshav Gedera, south of Rehovot. Moshe remained there for only a few weeks, however, as he finally decided to join the Settlement Police.

At Moshe's graduation I became friends with one of the girls who had arrived from Turkey two years earlier. Her group was also graduating, and they were preparing to found a kibbutz of their own. I told this girl, whose name was Meira, that I had decided to leave Tel Aviv. Jobs were scarce under the British Mandate, especially after the war when veterans were coming back onto the labor market, and it was impossible to earn much money. I explained that I was planning to go to Ashdot Ya'acov, a large secular kibbutz in the Jordan Valley. Meira said that she was not interested in going to start a new settlement, and she asked me if I thought she might be accepted at Ashdot. I told her that I would talk to the kibbutz secretary and let her know. A few days later, I visited the kibbutz and managed to get us accepted on a one-year trial basis. I relayed this message to Meira and we decided to give Ashdot Ya'acov a try.

With one thousand members, Ashdot Ya'acov was one of the largest kibbutzim in the country. It belonged to the Labor Party movement. The kibbutz owned a canning factory and one of the largest farm fisheries in Palestine, and it even employed some specialized labor from Haifa. One of my reasons for choosing this kibbutz was its well-equipped machine shop, in which I hoped to get some valuable experience.

At Ashdot Ya'acov I was given lodging with two other fellows about my age. One was a lathe operator in the machine shop and the other worked on a tractor and was a member of the Palmakh, the special attack unit of the Haganah. My friend Meira was assigned to work in the sewing room.

The cultural life of the kibbutz was rich and rewarding. We enjoyed movies once a week as well as plays and other performances. The library had many interesting books, and I was constantly reading. The books that I read gave me the inspiration to make a record of my experiences while they were still fresh in my memory. I had some notes that I had written earlier in Russian, so I translated them into Hebrew and thus began writing my story.

In the machine shop I worked alongside an elderly man named Abraham. Mr. Abraham was an old hand on the kibbutz, having been there since its inception thirty years earlier. Our first job was to help with the construction of bunkers on a hill across from the fish pools. The pools were next to the Yarmuk River, which was the border with Trans-Jordan. We had to build two bulletproof doors for these bunkers. After this was done, I helped build automatic presses to squeeze the juice from oranges. But I didn't spend all of my time working in the shop. During the harvest season, everybody helped out until the crops were in. On the weekends we would visit other kibbutzim such as Daganya A and B and Afikim. We also made trips to Tiberias and we swam in the Kinneret.

I had been in Eretz Israel for only three years, but it seemed a lifetime. I was now fluent in Hebrew, I had explored the land, and I was a contributing member of a well-established kibbutz. There was no doubt: I had become a Sabra.

Chapter Eight

The War Clouds Gather

Life on the kibbutz had its own steady rhythm, but the country as a whole was in turmoil. It was now 1946 and the British were waging undeclared war on us. They brought in over 100,000 paratroopers in red berets whom we nicknamed Kalaniyot ("Poppy Flowers"). These troops were needed, we were told, to defend the colonial office as well as British lives and property. They had been dispatched in response to terrorist attacks by Jews who were attempting to force the British out of Palestine.

Most Jews saw the departure of the British as an important goal, especially because they were refusing to allow survivors of the Holocaust to enter the country. The terrorism against the British was the work of three groups. The most extreme one, and the smallest, was the Lekhi—the Lokhamey Kherut Israeli Freedom Fighters, also known as the Stern Gang. The second group was a little larger than the first and less extreme. It had big national aspirations, and claimed that both sides of the Jordan River belonged historically to Israel. This group, the Etzel or Irgun Zvai Le'umi ("National Military Organization"), is today better known simply as the Irgun. The third group was the one I belonged to, the Haganah. Practically every kibbutz I knew of was full of Haganah members, and the same was true of many of the youth organizations in the cities.

The Irgun and the Lekhi attacked British military and administrative installations or staged ambushes against British soldiers. The Haganah was more subtle. It helped to arrange for Jews who had survived the Holocaust to sail to Palestine, even though they were forbidden to enter by the British. Every time the British Navy encountered an "illegal" vessel, they captured it and shipped the refugees to yet another detention camp in Cyprus. Many of these poor souls had already experienced the horrors of the German death camps and concentration camps. The Haganah hoped that the British treatment of refugees would speak for itself, and that world opinion and political pressure might help to break the British blockade. If a ship managed to slip past the British blockade, however, the Haganah would arrange to guide it to a safe location on the shore and would help to disperse the passengers before they could be rounded up by a British patrol. In some cases, it was necessary to ambush a patrol that was about to capture refugees. For the most part, however, the Haganah tried not to take British lives unless it was necessary to do so for self-defense.

The Haganah also sent operatives to different parts of the world to secure weapons of all sorts and to smuggle them into the country. In addition, many machine shops in various kibbutzim were able to manufacture parts for small arms that would later be assembled for Haganah use.

One Saturday—which later came to be known as "Shabbat Hashkhora" (Black Saturday)—my kibbutz, Ashdot Ya'acov, was raided by British soldiers. It was a beautiful morning, and I had overslept. I jumped out of bed only to find that I was alone. It was the season when grapes were being harvested, so I figured that everybody must be out in the vineyard. I was on my way to the vineyard when two British paratroopers jumped out from behind a bush with their Sten guns at the ready, screaming something I could not understand. They indicated that I was to walk in the direction of an open tent

At the tent I was handed over to a British officer who spoke broken Hebrew. He asked me my name, and I told him. The officer checked my name against a list that he had in front of him, and then ordered a soldier to escort me to a barbed-wire pen near the gate. In the pen there were several men who had been hired to work for the kibbutz. It seemed strange to me that I was the only kibbutz member in the holding pen.

I later found out that the kibbutz members had been told to remain silent when asked for their names, in part so as to protect the identity of Haganah members. Because I was new in the kibbutz, however, that directive had not yet been conveyed to me. I did not want to be seen as a traitor, and I had a good excuse for my behavior. Even so, many later asked me why I was separated from the other members of the kibbutz.

After detaining all the males from Ashdot Ya'acov, the soldiers entered the kibbutz grounds with electronic detectors to search for arms. Several soldiers passed out from heat stroke and were taken away by a Red Cross Military ambulance. A soldier who was guarding the pen I was in discharged a round into the ground. I don't know whether he did so on purpose, but an officer immediately escorted him away under guard.

The British found no arms in our kibbutz. This was because we had some very well-concealed sliks. They also failed to find a list of names that my roommate had hidden in the exhaust pipe of a Caterpillar tractor. My group was released after the search, but about a third of the kibbutz members were shipped off to a camp at Rafiakh in the northern Sinai for further interrogation. They were returned several days later. In the meantime, we were left short-handed, and everyone had to work extra hard to keep the kibbutz running.

The British conducted searches all over the country on Black Saturday. They were unfortunately more successful in other places than they were at Ashdot Ya'acov, and they managed to confiscate many much-needed weapons. Kibbutz Ganigar, near Haifa, was most unlucky. There the British discovered a large cache of arms, including mortars and machine guns. These sorts of weapons were very hard to come by.

After Black Saturday we realized that the British would not leave Palestine without a fight. The underground war against them intensified, and more and more British soldiers were killed in ambushes and even in direct actions against their fortified facilities. The British headquarters in Jerusalem's King David Hotel were blown up, and several officers were killed. When British soldiers found it necessary to move about, they walked in groups of eight to ten. The entire Jewish population was hostile to them.

Two of my friends from Mikveh Israel, Moshe Olek and Aaron Fishelberg, came to visit me at Ashdot Ya'acov. They were scouting around for a kibbutz they might like to join. I told them exactly what life was like on a kibbutz, and doing so helped me to realize that I did not wish to remain at Ashdot. As it turns out, my friend Meira came to the same conclusion. She decided that she would go back home to her parents in Turkey.

I said goodbye to the many friends I had made on the kibbutz and apologized to the secretary for leaving. I told him it was not the fault of Ashdot Ya'acov; I just needed to try something else. He said that he understood, but hated to see me go. The kibbutz, he told me, needed me more than Tel Aviv did.

I still had some money I had saved from my previous stay in Tel Aviv. This would help me get by for a while. I took the bus to Tel Aviv the next day. A friend of mine found a temporary place for me to sleep—a cot in his sister's patio. The place was in a run-down area near the Shouk Hacarmel Street on the outskirts of Yafo.

Asher Halpern, my former roommate from Tel Aviv, was employed by a contractor who owned two concrete-mixing machines that he leased out to construction sites. Asher felt he owed me a favor because I had helped him to get a job in the lock factory where I was employed when I first lived in Tel Aviv. Asher's job was to drive the machines to construction sites and operate them. I was hired to help him until I learned to operate and take care of the mixers, at which point I would be able to run the machines myself. Much of my time was spent dispersing the concrete on the construction site by repeatedly filling and emptying a rickshaw-type wheel-barrow.

Zvi, the owner of the concrete mixers, had had a heart problem, so he did the administrative tasks while Asher and I did the physical labor. For that I was paid 30 colonial pounds a month, or about $2.80 a day. It was virtually slave labor, but jobs were hard to come by.

After two nights on the cot in my friend's sister's house, I found another place. I was assisted by yet another classmate of mine from Mikveh Israel, Shimon Kupfershnidt. Shimon was rooming with the Goldstein family and said that they were looking for a boarder. Mrs.Goldstein lived in a three-bedroom house on Hanegev Street on the border of Tel Aviv and Yafo. Her two older children already had their own families, but Asher, her youngest, was still at home. Asher was about seventeen. He was a nice looking, blond and blue-eyed kid who played the accordion, and he was happy to have another boarder close to his age. Mr. Goldstein was a self-employed carpenter with a shop of his own in the back of the house. I paid five pounds per month for lodging, including Friday and Saturday evening meals with the family. I had a bed and mattress in the hallway, and I usually went to bed after everyone else had gone to sleep.

I led a bachelor's life and was relatively content. I would certainly have preferred to work in mechanics or in a machine shop, but those sorts of jobs were hard to come by. I also wanted to further my education. Unfortunately I could not afford the luxury of paying tuition, nor could I work irregular hours. I had no relatives to lean on, so I simply had to be happy with what I had.

Looking back, I see that I did not realize how dangerous my work was. In order to prepare for pouring the concrete, Asher and I had to build a scaffold made up of two-by-fours nailed together to double their thickness. We would then fashion beams out of these four-by-fours, extending them sometimes to the height of six stories. The two beams then had to be attached to the frame of the building. On the level where the concrete was to be poured we had to build a bridge capable of receiving a five or six cubic-foot bucket of concrete. To get the bucket up to the bridge, we had to carry up a block that weighed about 150 lbs. and attach it to the top of the scaffold. We would then lower two steel cables from the block and attach them to the bottom of the scaffold. These cables allowed the concrete bucket to be guided up by a winch attached to the mixer. We had no gloves, no hard hats, no goggles, and no dust masks, and the bucket was raised by a machine operator standing under the scaffold with no protective gear whatsoever. More than once, the cable broke and the bucket came tumbling down and flattened like a pancake when it hit the ground.

There were other accidents, too. I was once carrying the steel block up the scaffold and the board on which I was standing cracked under the weight. I was able to jump clear in time, which was lucky because I was five stories above the ground. Another time the entire scaffold collapsed. We always used materials provided by the building contractor, and in this case the two-by-fours were old and had been used many times.

Occasionally the machines broke down, and I had to run all over town to find replacement parts. When I was unsuccessful, we had to cannibalize one machine in order to repair the other. The one-cylinder kerosene engines had to be cranked by hand, and when they backfired they could sprain a man's wrist. Sometimes the engines simply refused to start. When things went wrong, the contractor would scream—and rightly so, as he was paying the help by the hour and nothing was happening. At times like these the sparks would fly, and sometimes we came close to blows. In spite of all these drawbacks, we somehow always managed to get the job done.

We once poured concrete for a semicircular three-story building with a basement near Abu Kabir on the outskirts of Tel Aviv on Hertzel Street. Asher and I started the job on a Thursday and finished at noon on Friday. We worked non-stop, and took four days off to rest.

I dated girls off and on, but only when I had enough money to take them to a movie or to buy a soft drink. To set up a date I had to arrange in advance to meet at a certain time and place. This was because only rich people and businesses had phones. Often a surprise curfew would be imposed by the British. If you were with a girl, you had to hurry home and let your date fend for herself.

One Saturday night I was out with a group of friends. We were walking past King George Square on Allenby Street when a group of fellows opened fire right in front of us with semiautomatic handguns. We scattered instantly, and after it was over we found seven soldiers lying in the street, bleeding profusely. One soldier had dragged himself and his rifle into a storefront with his rifle to take cover. Several men quickly collected the guns that had been dropped by dying or wounded soldiers, and then scattered in different directions. Needless to say, everyone tried to get way from the scene as fast as possible. I saw the faces of the soldiers for just an instant and they looked black to me, so I assumed they were Africans. The morning news, however, reported that they were British and that the attack had been carried out by the Lekhi.

I had not seen my brother Moshe since his graduation from Mikveh Israel, almost a year earlier. As if he were reading my mind, he showed up one Saturday in the autumn of 1946 for a visit. I almost did not recognize him. He had shot up in height and was nearly a full head taller than me. As luck would have it, a curfew was proclaimed for Tel Aviv at the exact time he came to visit. Moshe had to be back in Gedara, and in any case I had no place for him to stay. I decided to take him out of Tel Aviv by skirting the British road-blocks. The curfew boundary was Abu Kabir where I had once worked, so I knew the sidestreets whereby one could avoid the British patrols. After I got Moshe to Abu Kabir, he was able to catch a bus home. As for me, I had to return home by way of the rooftops in order to avoid getting caught.

The next time Moshe came to visit was in the summer of 1947—and surprise of surprises, he was wearing the uniform of the Settlement Mounted Police, complete with an Australian hat. He looked tall and handsome in his uniform. We went out on the town and had a good time together. He told me all about his training, including how he learned to ride horseback, handle rifles, and operate Lewis machine guns. He also told me that most of his classmates from Mikveh Israel had joined the Settlement Police. I was worried about him, however, because I knew that even though the Settlement Police was administered by the British, it was largely a cover for the Haganah.

Throughout 1946 and until the British left the country, the three militant Jewish groups caused plenty of trouble for our colonial masters. Not a day went by without some attack on the British administration. The British soldiers garrisoned themselves behind barbed wire and ventured out only in force. The Royal Navy was tied down at sea to enforce the blockade. More and more ships and small boats were captured trying to break the blockade. Meanwhile, the detention camps on Cyprus filled up and new ones had to be built. All of these conditions put political and financial strain on the British. This strain was increased in 1947 by the way the British handled the 4500 refugees who had come to Palestine on board the Haganah ship *Exodus*, an incident that provoked world outcry against their treatment of refugees.[1]

The refugee situation was especially close to my heart because my parents were among the many who suffered as a result of the British blockade of Palestine. My parents left the Soviet Union in 1946 in order to return to Poland. (They were accompanied by Aunt Frieda, but not by Uncle Wolf, who had run off with a Russian Christian woman in Uzbekistan and was never heard from again.) The Poles were often hostile to returning Jews, especially when they were asked to give back property that they had seized while the Jewish owners were away. In fact, there were many instances in which Jews who had survived the Holocaust were murdered by Poles after the war. My cousin Wladek Tauber appears to have been one such victim. When the war ended, Wladek and his wife and children came back from the Soviet Union to their home in Warsaw. According to Wladek's brother Moniek, Wladek established himself in some capacity as a civic official and was subsequently poisoned by a Polish rival. Wladek's family was ultimately able to leave Poland, and settled in Israel in 1951.

My parents made it to Poland but did not return to Chelm. A friend of theirs who had gone back to Chelm informed them that there was nothing left there to return to. Luckily, they met some Haganah agents who helped them to join a group that was to be guided to Palestine. My parents agreed to go because they wanted to be reunited with their sons. They were taken to Czechoslovakia and then to Germany, where they were interned in a displaced persons camp for several months. While at the camp, my mother found her sister Gitl and Gitl's son Arie and daughter Zelda, all of whom had survived the extermination camps. Gitl's husband Moshe was killed by the Germans, and her daughter Henya, a beautiful teenager, was used as a sex slave by the German soldiers and did not survive. Gitl's third daughter, Malka, escaped death by posing as a Pole.

From the DP camp in Germany my parents were taken to Italy to await a boat to Palestine. They joined several hundred people on an old fishing boat. The boat was captured by the British and my parents were interned in Cyprus.

Eventually the British were forced to bring the issue of Palestine to the United Nations. In the meantime the British forces in Palestine, knowing that eventually they would have to leave, abandoned some of their fortified police stations and turned them over to Arab bands. The neighboring Arab countries began to supply arms to the local Arabs, and they were given additional arms by the British.

The whole country was in turmoil. There was constant sniper fire from the prayer towers of mosques, and there were frequent shootings on the fringes of Tel Aviv, especially in Yafo, Abu Kabir in the south, and Menshiye in the west. Asher and I could no longer work on some of the buildings for fear of sniper fire. The Haganah and some units from the other militant groups were posted in strategic areas to defend Jews. We had a chronic shortage of arms and ammunition, but the Arabs seemed to have plenty of both. But we did have a secret weapon—our determination to survive and to bring our families to Eretz Israel.

The Palestine problem finally came to a vote in the United Nations. The question before the General Assembly was whether to partition Palestine and thereby establish an independent Jewish state. On the day of the vote I was awakened sometime after midnight by shouts coming from the street. We all got up and went outside. A large crowd was assembled at the King George Square, where a loudspeaker on a balcony was relaying the news from Lake Success, New York, where the voting took place. When the final count was complete, the crowd let out a tremendous shout of joy and began to sing Hatikvah, "The Hope," a song that would become the national anthem of the new state of Israel:

Kol ode balevav P'nimah / Nefesh Yehudi homiyah / Ulfa'atey mizrach kadimah / Ayin l'tzion tzofiyah. / Ode lo avdah tikvatenu / Hatikvah bat shnot alpayim: / L'hiyot am chofshi b'artzenu / Eretz Tzion v'Yerushalayim.

As long as the Jewish spirit is yearning deep in the heart,

With eyes turned toward the East, looking toward Zion,

Then our hope—the two-thousand-year-old hope—will not be lost:

To be a free people in our land, the land of Zion and Jerusalem.

I was filled with emotion. After two thousand years, we were once again going to have our own home. It was November 29, 1947.

The state of Israel was founded on May 14, 1948. By the next day, Israel was under attack by the Egyptians, Syrians, Lebanese, Jordanians, and Iraqis. This was the beginning of the War of Independence, which lasted until the summer of 1949. But the Jews of Palestine began to fight for survival many months before the War of Independence started.

Events moved swiftly after the partition vote in November of 1947. The Arabs of Palestine responded to the vote by rioting and, wherever possible, by attacking Jews. Most of my friends were called up by the Haganah to take up arms. The Palmakh, the elite core of the Haganah, became very active in establishing defense perimeters in various farm settlements, especially those close to Arab villages. The British retreated from dangerous or unstable areas and did nothing to keep law and order. The neighboring Arab states began to infiltrate irregular forces to organize the local Arabs and supply them with arms. These bands of infiltrators forced even those Arabs who were friendly to their Jewish neighbors to become hostile on pain of being executed as traitors to the Arab cause. They also encouraged whole villages to flee to neighboring Arab states and get out of the way of battle. Villagers were told that after the regular Arab armies had invaded and defeated the Jews, they could come back and take their pick of Jewish farms and property. Thus began a mass exodus of many Arabs from Israel. These are the people whose children and grandchildren now live in refugee camps in Gaza, Lebanon, and other Arab states.

Jerusalem became isolated and the only supply road leading to the city from Tel Aviv was regularly attacked by Arab bands that controlled the high ground in the mountains. My brother Moshe was dispatched to escort convoys to Jerusalem and was involved in a number of skirmishes. To protect the drivers in the convoys, the cabs and engines of the trucks were fortified with armored steel plates. This stopped bullets, but did nothing to mitigate the effects of landmines.

In March of 1948 I received my orders to report for active duty.

NOTES

1. The Jews on board the *Exodus* were arrested and sent to France and then to a displaced persons camp in Germany. Golda Meir writes the following about the incident: "If I live to be a hundred, I shall never erase from my mind the gruesome picture of hundreds of British soldiers in full combat dress, bearing and using clubs, pistols and grenades against the wretched refugees of the *Exodus*, 400 of whom were pregnant women determined to give birth to their babies in Palestine. Nor will I ever be able to forget the revulsion with which I heard that these people were actually going to be shipped back, like animals in their wire cages, to DP camps in the one country that symbolized the graveyard of European Jewry." *My Life* (New York: G.P. Putnam's Sons, 1975), 207.

Chapter Nine

A Fight for Independence

On March 5, 1948, Asher Halpern and I reported to the induction base on the outskirts of Tel Aviv. I did not know whether this induction was to be kept secret or not, since the British were still in the country. At the base we were told that this was the beginning of the transformation of the Haganah to the new IDF (Israel Defense Force), which would be the army of the new Jewish state.

Asher and I were processed, registered and assigned identification numbers. Mine was 5712, which indicated that I was in one of the first groups of soldiers to be activated for duty.

For two days we marched and hiked to get in shape. On the third day a review party came to visit our group for the purpose of selecting draftees for the various branches of the IDF. We were lined up for a roll call and looked over. One of the men in charge of selection was, I believe, a South African Jewish volunteer. This man asked about my trade, and I replied that I was a mechanic and machinist. Another man in the selection group wanted me in the Military Police, but the South African insisted that I be drafted into the Air Force, which was then known as the "Air Service." Asher was sent to the Northern Command to fight in Haifa and the Galilee

I was issued a uniform—a used Australian army jacket and pants, but no hat. The shirt, socks, and underwear were my own. I was housed in a hotel on Allenby Street near the sea. My friends could not believe my luck, since most of them had to live in barracks or tents. I knew I would be moved eventually, but for the time being I enjoyed myself.

At the time of my induction into the IDF there were no insignia of any sort, and there were no official ranks. Just as in the Haganah, everyone knew who the commanding officers were, and what degree of responsibility each one had.

The Air Service or Sheyrut Avir was actually a branch of the Haganah that had been active since November of 1947. I was assigned to the Palmakh Air Unit, which consisted of graduates from the Aviron flying school and veterans from the British Royal Air Force (RAF). In the beginning my unit had only 11 aircraft, a motley collection of Tiger Moths, RWD13s, Zlins, Taylorcrafts, Austers, Seabees and two twin-engine Rapides. About the time when I became an airman we bought 21 more Austers from the British. The Auster, which was about the size of a Piper Cub, was nicknamed the "Primus" after the kerosene burners used for cooking in most homes.

I was assigned to the Sdeh Dov airfield in north Tel Aviv. Sdeh Dov was a small civilian airfield with one short runway oriented east to west. (The prevailing winds almost always come in from the sea in the west.) The airfield had a small shack for storing tools that also served as an office. To the north of us was the Reading Power Station that supplied electricity to Tel Aviv. Apart from these structures, the rest of the landscape around the airfield consisted of sand dunes.

Although the British were officially still in command of Palestine, they were getting ready to leave and did nothing to preserve law and order. Infiltrators from the neighboring Arab States, primarily Syria and Iraq, organized local Arab guerrillas to harass and kill Jewish farmers and do as much damage as possible to Jewish defenses. The Jewish population in the countryside and towns regularly repelled Arab attacks with the help of the Haganah and Palmakh. Our mission in the Air Service was to help supply and defend areas in which fighting broke out.

Part of my job was to service the Primus aircraft and keep them flying. Since I was new to airplanes I had to learn fast. Fortunately we had some veteran volunteers from the U.S., Canada, and the RAF to show us what needed to be done. I was also helped by the fact that the Auster is a simple aircraft and not very difficult to maintain.

The Auster was a civilian aircraft, and we needed to adapt it to military use. It wasn't long before someone came up with an idea for installing bomb racks on these small airplanes. We soon built racks and mounted them next to the wheels. Because of its limited size and power, the Auster could carry only 20 to 50 kilogram bombs. From then on the Primus was elevated to the rank of "Bomber."

The Air Service flew many missions to resupply the Gush Etzion region and ward off attacks on the road to Jerusalem. Kfar Etzion was the kibbutz where many of my classmates from Mikveh Israel had settled in 1946. The situation there was very critical. The area was predominantly Arab, which made it very difficult to get to the kibbutz. The mountainous terrain only compounded the difficulty. On one occasion an entire compliment of Palmakh men were ambushed on their way to help Gush Etzion and never made it through. Every time we sent an Auster to drop supplies I wished we could have sent more, since each plane could carry very little in addition to the pilot. But we did the best we could to help out.

Gush Etzion fell in May of 1948. The Arab Legion of Trans-Jordan was led by the former British officer John Bagot Glubb, known to his soldiers as Glubb Pasha, and was outfitted with modern equipment supplied by the British. This was more than Kfar Etzion could handle. The kibbutz had only rifles and some light machine guns. Yet the kibbutz fell only after the defenders ran out of ammunition and resorted to throwing rocks at the attackers. Three defenders were taken prisoner, and these only because they were wounded. The rest were killed outright. The prisoners of war were two women and one man by the name of Arie Kleinzahler. Arie became a friend of mine after he was repatriated from Trans-Jordan. He told me that his older brother Dov was killed in Kfar Etzion. Had I gone to Kfar Etzion with my classmates, I probably would have died there in 1948.

One of our greatest challenges in the months before the War of Independence began was to keep possession of the road connecting Tel Aviv with Jerusalem. The survival of Jerusalem depended on these forty miles of two-lane highway. The road passed almost entirely through Arab territory in the barren hills of Judea. From these hills the Arabs could shoot down at anything that moved on the highway. Many Jews died on this road, and some of the mountain bunkers and fortresses in the hills above the road changed hands many times in the course of battle.

I had an old friend from Mikveh Israel named Malka whose sister lived in Jerusalem. Malka related to me the hardship her sister had to endure between January and May 1948. In addition to shortages of food and water, the Jewish section of the city had to endure constant bombardment. British troops occasionally helped to repel Arab irregulars from the neighboring Arab states, but for the most part the Haganah and Palmakh were on their own. The British also turned over some police fortresses to the Arabs. And while the Jewish population had to abide by the arms embargo imposed on them by the United Nations, Palestinian Arabs were getting all the arms they needed from neighboring Arab states. The situation was desperate, but the Jews had determination and courage and were ready to die for their homeland.

Our little Air Service Austers flew non-stop missions. Some of them never came back, but this only increased our determination to succeed.

I was not at Sdeh Dov for long. Around the end of March 1948, I was transferred to Sarona, a former German colony in Tel Aviv that we inherited from the British. During World War II the British evacuated the German residents of the colony to Australia and established a base there. When we took it over from the British, the Air Service (which in May of 1948 would become the Israel Defense Force/ Air Force, or IDF/ AF) made Sarona its headquarters. I was assigned to the aircraft engine repair shop, which we set up in a wine cellar. There were about eight of us who claimed to be mechanics. One of the men who had served in the RAF was supposed to have had experience in engine overhaul, but the rest of us were sorely in need of training. So when we received a radial engine that belonged to a DC3, we decided to take it apart and put it back together. I did not know what I was doing but I hoped that the other fellows did. At any rate, we finished the engine with the help of various manuals. All of us gathered around it and took a snapshot of the first engine "repair" in the Air Service. However, the rebuilt engine would not start.

It is hard to believe that the famous Israeli Air Force grew from such humble beginnings.

On several occasions I tried to find out what my brother Moshe was doing. I was very concerned about his welfare. I knew he had been trained to drive an armored truck, and that he was playing a part in what would later come to be known as the "Battle of the Roads"—the ongoing effort to keep open certain key roads that ran through areas populated by Palestinian Arabs. But I was never able to get details of Moshe's whereabouts.

I finally heard from Moshe in April of 1948. Starting in late 1947, Moshe told me, he escorted supply trucks to Jerusalem in a pickup truck with a machine gun mounted on its bed. His duty was to fight off ambushes and Arab snipers alongside the road. In January of 1948, he was assigned to a 1938 Ford truck that had been fitted with steel plates for protection against sniper fire. Moshe told me that the truck was so heavy that the mechanical brakes were almost useless on a downhill run. In order to stop the truck he had to use all of his strength to press down on the brake pedal.

In April and May of 1948, Moshe was involved in heroic actions while helping to break the Arab blockade of Jerusalem. The following are excerpts from a letter about these events that he wrote many years later.

"I left the police station in Rehovot in my 'armored' truck about midnight with eight of my buddies and our sergeant. Behind me was a truck loaded with machine gun and rifle ammunition, mortars, shells and other supplies. Our destination was Maaleh Hakhamisha or Kiryat Anavim south of Jerusalem, where Itzhak Rabin's Harrell unit was to be resupplied for the upcoming attack against the Arab stronghold Kastel. Kastel had a commanding view of the road to Jerusalem and was harassing the supply lines to the city.

It was a moonless night and I could hardly see the road through the slits of· the armor. One of the soldiers volunteered to sit on the left fender of the truck so he could guide me and also watch for landmines. We had to maintain silence as much as possible so as not to give away our position to the nearby Latrun fortress, which had been handed to the Arabs by the British. After we passed La-trun I turned towards the mountains onto an obscure donkey trail. The trail was very narrow. On my right was the mountainside and on my left was a ravine. The trail was full of potholes, and I was guiding my truck slowly from one pothole to the next, one wheel at a time. Suddenly the moon appeared from behind the clouds and I noticed a pile of rocks laid across the road. My sergeant crawled out towards the rock pile through the security door in the floor of the truck. As he came closer to the pile he noticed a sign that said "mines" in Arabic. Appar-ently the Arabs meant to warn their own people and didn't think the Jews could read Arabic. Rather then move any rock and accidentally detonate any mines, we elected to place charges and blow them up. The explosions woke up the Arabs and they opened fire, not in our direction but in the direction of the main road.

We continued on from one pothole to the next very carefully. The vehicle be-hind me was a new one, driven by the owner who had been mobilized along with his truck. Rather then follow my tracks, the driver was trying to avoid the pot-holes in order to preserve his truck. All of a sudden we were rocked by a tremen-dous explosion. We were covered with dust and showered by flying rocks. To my horror I discovered that the entire front end of the truck behind me had been blown off, apparently by a mine. Fortunately no one was injured other then the driver, who was in shock. We were very lucky that none of the ordinance in the truck had exploded.

We quickly transferred all of the ordinance to my truck and continued towards Jerusalem. We knew how important these supplies were to Mr. Rabin and his Harrell unit.

Several kilometers from Kiryat Anavim we came to a broad ditch that was dug across the road. I knew that my truck could not make it across so we con-tacted the Harrell unit by radio and informed them about the situation. The Har-rell command ordered us to wait and told us that help was on the way. Shortly afterwards a truck showed up loaded with fifty gallon drums. The drums were placed into the ditch and we were able to cross it and arrive safely in Kiryat Anavim. There my truck and my buddies were attached temporarily to the Har-rell unit because the road back to Rehovot had been closed by the Arabs.

. . . While I was attached to the Harrell brigade we received orders to proceed to Kfar Etzion in order to open the blockade to the Gush Etzion area and to bring in badly needed supplies. We passed through Beit Lahatz, advancing in the di-rection of Kfar Etzion. All the way we were taking fire from the surrounding Arab villages. In spite of the heavy fire my armored truck reached King Solomon's Pools. From there I could see the kibbutz on the hill. I had many friends there with whom I had gone to school in Mikveh. I could not advance farther because the road was blocked by a huge barricade made up of large boul-ders. In addition the men from Harrell were taking substantial losses. We gave Kfar Etzion fire support as long as we could. An Auster from my brother's Air Service came in and dropped some cans loaded with explosives mixed with nails right on top of the Arabs. My armored truck took many hits and all four tires were punctured. We were ordered to retreat back to Ramat Rachel near Jerusalem. There were too many Arabs and too few Jews. In addition the Arab Legion from Trans-Jordan, which was equipped and guided by British officers, was fighting alongside the hordes of Arab irregulars. Thus Kfar Etzion fell and all my classmates perished. We retreated with tears and clenched fists. I felt in my bones that someday we would take Gush Etzion back. In June of 1967, during the Six Day War, we did just that."

In April of 1948 I received orders to transfer some equipment from Sarona to the newly vacated RAF base in Ekron, which was later named Tel Nof. This had been the largest RAF base in the Middle East. I made the journey along with seven other men. I was given a Luger pistol and several hand grenades just in case we ran into trouble.

To get to Ekron we had to go south from Sarona past Kibbutz Givat Brenner and then head east for about a mile. When we reached Ekron we found one platoon from the Givaty Brigade guarding the base. The platoon had one homemade armored truck and one Spandau water-cooled machine gun dating from World War I. The ammunition belt for the machine gun was locally made and jammed every other round. Besides the machine gun the men were equipped with rifles and Sten guns. Luckily, the Arabs in the surrounding villages did not know how poorly equipped we were. At night we made a lot of noise and drove the armored vehicle all over the place to make the Arabs believe that there was at least a battalion present.

We Air Service men had been asked to report on the condition of the base. It was a huge base with six large hangars, a control tower, and many workshops. Much of the equipment had been removed by the British when they vacated Ekron, but they left behind a substantial salvage yard and nine broken-down Wellington Bombers. There were also a couple of Spitfire fuselages with no wings.

Gradually the Air Service and then the IDF/ AF established itself in Tel Nof, and the shops and hangars were refurbished. On several occasions during the War of Independence Egyptian Air Force Spitfires attacked the base and hit a couple of empty hangars. The shrapnel from the explosions made the corrugated steel walls of the hangars look like wire-mesh sifters. Most of these attacks came at night, and several of the Egyptian Spitfires were shot down by ground fire. This gave us Air Force mechanics a chance to work on some of the downed aircraft, which we planned to refurbish when we got spare parts.

My commanding officer, Colonel Rabin (no relation to General Yitzhak Rabin), called me into his office when I got back in Sarona and asked me if I would like to go to school to learn aircraft mechanics. Without hesitation I replied in the affirmative. I felt that this was a unique opportunity to improve my skills. The school was the prestigious Technion in Haifa, about eighty miles north of Tel Aviv. The Technion was considered to be one of the best technical colleges in the world. I received my transfer papers to the Technion and reported to the director of the course. We were given some entry exams in arithmetic, algebra, and a few other subjects. I had a little problem with algebra because the last time I had had this subject was in Siberia, and I did not remember much of it. But the school director overlooked this weakness because I did so well on the other parts of the exam.

Our group was named BAHAT II (a Hebrew acronym for Technical Air School, no. II). We received lodging and food in a top-quality hotel called Hadar Hacarmel, which was situated on top of Mount Carmel overlooking the Bay of Haifa. There I met three other airmen with whom I became close friends, Avraham Nussbaum, Ze'ev Sollel, and Naftali Ben-Shimon. We became a close-knit group, and all of us eventually made important contributions to the Air Force. The courses in aircraft mechanics were divided into theory and practice. Some of the subjects I had studied previously, but most of it was new to me and very interesting. I tried hard to learn everything thoroughly and to be the best student I could.

When I arrived in Haifa the Arab part of the city had just been liberated. The Haganah had also liberated a large facility in the bay next to the airport. Our class at the Technion was assigned the task of cleaning up debris and preparing the area for a permanent technical training base for the Air Force. The facility was a former school, so it did not take us very long to clean up the place and continue our classes. We moved from the hotel into the school, and in addition to our studies we now also had to engage in guard duty night and day.

One night when I was guarding the perimeter next to the airfield a twin engine airplane flew over the city. We all assumed that we were under attack. The sirens sounded and the plane began to draw ground fire. The plane circled the city and then came in for a landing at our airfield, stopping near the school building. Several cars were in pursuit of the aircraft as it landed. When the plane came to a stop I ran over to it, my Sten gun ready for any eventuality. To my surprise the pilot climbed down from the Mosquito fighter-bomber madder than a hornet. He walked over to me and screamed "Are you guys nuts trying to shoot me down!" As it turned out this pilot was a foreign volunteer delivering a fighter plane to the Air Force, but no one had informed us about any such delivery. The pilot was lucky that he did not get shot down, especially since it seemed like everyone in town was firing at his aircraft.

The State of Israel was born on May 14, 1948 by proclamation of David Ben-Gurion, Prime Minister and head of the provisional government. I watched from Mount Carmel as the British flag in the Haifa port was lowered for the last time, and I saw the boat carrying the British High Commissioner Sir Allan Gordon Cunningham make its way toward the Royal Navy cruiser *Euryalus*, which was waiting in the distance.

On the same day the armies of five Arab countries, which were already poised for attack on the borders of Israel, launched their assault against the Jewish state. Syria, Lebanon, and Iraq struck in the north, the Arab Legion of Trans-Jordan in the east, and Egypt in the south. We mobilized all of our national resources to repel those armies. The kibbutzim in the north stopped the Syrian tanks with Molotov cocktails and trenches and many acts of bravery. But the Arab Legion was more successful than their allies in the north. They captured the Old City of Jerusalem and penetrated into Judea and Samaria, in the region later known as the West Bank. The Egyptians captured most of the Negev Desert in the south and reached Kibbutz Negba and Yad Mordechai, about twenty miles from Tel Aviv.

During the first weeks of the war I continued my studies at the Technion. In one of my classes in the engine shop I was using a dial indicator to measure the bore of an engine cylinder when I heard someone call my name. I looked up and could not believe my eyes. In the doorway stood my brother Moshe with a Sten gun slung on his shoulder. Behind him was my father. I ran to them and we hugged each other as though we would never let go. My father kept repeating my name and saying "My son, my son!" I received permission to take off to visit my family. Moshe had been granted forty-eight hours leave from his unit to find me and visit our parents.

It had not been easy for my parents to get to Israel. When their rule in Palestine was coming to an end, the British ordered all Jews in detainment on the island of Cyprus to be released. Thus my parents, having being captured in 1947 by the British while trying to enter Palestine and subsequently interned in Cyprus, were released and came to Israel. My mother had the address of Moshe's unit of the Settlement Police in Rehovot and set out to try to find him. At the time my parents were in a refugee camp in Pardes Hannah, about 40 miles from Rehovot. My mother came to Moshe's military base just at the time he was fighting in Kfar Etzion. The base commander showed her my brother's tent and bunk and said that her son would be back soon. He did not want to tell her that Moshe was in the midst of a battle. The commander ordered his driver to take my mother back to her camp in Pardes Hannah and assured her that as soon as Moshe returned he would send him to her. So it was. When Moshe came back he got in touch with the Air Force and was told where I was. Moshe checked out a jeep and went to see my parents and then took my father with him to come and get me.

All three of us drove up to my hotel so I could change clothes. When Moshe saw the hotel I was staying in he said to me "Now that's the way to

fight a war!" I replied that I was helping to build a force that would make his
job easy.

On the way to see my mother we passed a couple of British check points, but
they did not stop us. Moshe and I were fully armed, we were driving a military
jeep in a Jewish area, and the British were in any case preparing for departure.
My father filled me in on some details of their capture by the British navy. The
chartered fishing boat they had boarded in Italy was packed to the gills with
refugees. It took three miserable days for them to get within sight of the shores
of Palestine. When they were spotted by the British, a couple of frigates closed
in on their boat and squeezed it until they began to fear its boards would crack.
British sailors then boarded the vessel and towed it to Cyprus.

As we drove into the refugee camp in Pardes Hannah, we were surrounded
by curious onlookers. When we entered the barracks and someone pointed us
out to my mother, she came running and screaming "my children, my children." After a long and tearful embrace, we sat down to talk.

My parents had aged significantly and looked worn and tired. I frankly did
not feel as attached to them as I had when I left them six years earlier. Much
had happened since then. Moshe and I had grown up, we were engaged in a
war for our very survival, and battles were being fought all around us—in
some cases, only a few miles away. Moshe and I had the free spirit of Israelis,
while these newcomers had the visible stamp of the Jewish Diaspora. They
too would change in time. In the meanwhile I could not help but be aware of
the gulf that separated us.

While on Cyprus, my father had somehow gotten his hands on a bit of
leather and had fashioned a fine pair of shoes for me. He could only guess
how much my feet had grown, however, and the shoes proved to be too small.
To show my appreciation I wore the shoes a few times in his presence, but my
feet ached badly as a result.

The Jewish immigration agency was resettling all new arrivals in various
parts of the country in temporary "tent cities" pending permanent arrangements. I did not want my parents living in a tent. They had had enough, and
I wanted them to live in Tel Aviv. I used my savings to help them get settled,
making a down payment for an apartment on Kfar Giladi street. I also helped
my father find work in a shoe factory until he could establish himself on his
own. We moved them to Tel Aviv and I returned to Haifa.

I should mention that Aunt Frieda, who had been interned with my parents
in Cyprus, came with them to Israel but was not assigned to the camp at
Pardes Hannah. Frieda remained in Israel and remarried, and she and her husband opened a grocery store.

Back in Haifa, our group received orders to go to the newly-evacuated RAF
base in Ramat David to secure it and salvage anything we could for future use.

At that time we began to receive arms and Messerschmitt fighter planes that the Israeli government had purchased from Czechoslovakia. This was a godsend, as our army was in desperate need of more weapons and aircraft. I received a Beza heavy machine gun to help guard the base against possible air attack. I was itching to shoot at something, but fortunately nothing exciting came our way. At the base we were able to salvage much equipment in the shops. The British also left behind several damaged Spitfire fighter planes, which we prepared for the time when we could get spare parts to make them serviceable.

We finally finished our crash course in aircraft mechanics and were dispatched to various bases. I was ordered to return to Tel Nof.

The Air Force was beginning to take shape. Kfar Sirkin, which was north of Tel Aviv, became the base for our newly-acquired Me-109 Messerschmitt fighters. Our pilots were taught how to fly these planes by some Czech instructors, and before long had mastered the art of flying the Me-109. Most of the men who flew these planes had been RAF Spitfire pilots, so the transition was not particularly difficult for them.

The new Messerschmitts began to pay off immediately. On the night of May 29–30, 1948, four Me-109 pilots—Lou Lenart, Mordechai Kalibanski, Ari Cohen, and Ezer Weizmann (who later became chief of the IDF/ AF and President of Israel, and who was the nephew of Israel's first president, Chaim Weizmann)—single-handedly stopped the advance toward Tel Aviv of an Egyptian column of 500 vehicles. The four pilots were subjected to heavy anti-aircraft fire in the course of this action, and Cohen was killed. And on June 3, I happened to be strolling down Allenby Street when two Egyptian DC-3s flew over Tel Aviv intending to bomb the city. I heard the planes and the air-raid sirens, and as I looked up I saw a Messerschmitt dive and open fire on the two Egyptian bombers and shoot them down. Back at the base I found out that the planes had been shot down by Mody Allon, a pilot I knew.

I worked on most of the planes that came into Tel Nof for repair or maintenance. To service the various aircraft, I had to use three toolboxes with different sorts of tools: metric for the Messerschmitts, Whitworth for the British aircraft, and regular inch-system tools for the American planes. The Me-109 was one of the most difficult planes to service. The spark plugs on the no. 11 and 12 cylinders required special tools that I did not have. And there were other problems as well. The landing gear was anchored in the fuselage and was unusually narrow, which made the plane unstable when landing. This fact, and our pilots' inexperience with this type of aircraft, caused the Me-109s to crash occasionally. Another problem was the lack of spare parts. But somehow we managed to keep our aircraft flying.

Fortunately our agents abroad kept supplying us with arms and planes. We received three B-17 bombers with which we carried out air attacks on Cairo,

Rafa and El-Arish in the Sinai in retaliation for bombing raids on Tel Aviv. I recall being on alert to receive these planes for refueling during a bombing mission. The airfields lights were not functioning, so we lined the field with empty five-gallon cans filled with oil-permeated sand. On signal we ran down the field and lit those cans to show the planes where to land. We had several false alarms, when the planes failed to show up we ran to put out the fires. At last we received the planes and refueled them using hand pumps.

We were also able to buy some more Spitfires in Europe, and on one occasion received a flight of several Spitfires led by Ezer Weitzman. The trip across the Mediterranean Sea took five hours and required the use of auxiliary fuel tanks. When the planes landed in Tel Nof the engines were leaking oil all over. They were lucky to have made it across the water.

Throughout the war our workshops received some excellent technicians from among the new immigrants that were arriving every day from Europe and other lands. New volunteer pilots who had served in the RAF also continued to join the Air Force. Sy Feldman, with whom I later became a close friend, was one such pilot. Sy was one of the first RAF pilots to divert a German V-1 rocket. He did this by tipping the rocket into the English Channel with the wing of his Spitfire. For his bravery Sy was awarded a medal by King George.

Once the initial fog of war cleared, it became evident that Israel was beginning to prevail against the Arab forces. On the Syrian front in the Galilee, Hula, and Jordan Valley, Israelis overran Arab villages and smashed the invading armies. The factors that turned the war in Israel's favor included courage, daring, and imagination in the use of commando tactics such as surprise attacks. But perhaps the most important factor in our success was our superior motivation. The settlers and farmers of the kibbutzim were willing to die for the first independent Jewish state since the fall of Jerusalem to the Romans, but the Arab neighbors of Israel had no real reason to fight. Their soldiers came from across the borders to wage a war that was neither in their hearts nor in their personal interest.

The Arab plan had been to divide northern Israel between Syria and Iraq, to leave Jerusalem and Tel Aviv to King Abdullah of Trans-Jordan, and to give Egypt the southern part of the country. West Jerusalem held out in spite of all odds against the Arab Legion of Trans-Jordan. The Old City—the part of Jerusalem that is enclosed by ancient walls—caved in to the Arab Legion only after the Jews who were defending it were cut off and ran out of ammunition. The supply road to Jerusalem had been blocked, and the so-called "Burma Road," a makeshift path that bypassed the main road, was completed too late to save the Old City.

The Egyptians, invading from the south, aimed a two-prong attack at Tel Aviv and Jerusalem. They were stopped on the outskirts of Jerusalem in the suburb of Ramat Rakhel. The fierce battle involved hand-to-hand combat at times, and nearly every house in Ramat Rakhel was destroyed. Ramat Rakhel had been a beautiful place with lovely gardens and a view of both the Dead Sea and the city of Jerusalem. But when I visited it in 1949, the destruction wrought by war nearly broke my heart.

The inability of the Egyptians and Trans-Jordanians to conquer Jerusalem and to proceed with their plan to divide Israel deflated them on other fronts as well. On June 11 a cease fire was implemented, but on July 9 fighting resumed when the Arabs refused to extend the cease fire. However, the short truce period gave us time to regroup and resupply our units with better and newer equipment purchased from Czechoslovakia. Immediately after fighting resumed in July, our troops recaptured the Lod Airport, the largest civilian airport in Israel (which would later become the Ben-Gurion International Airport). The attack was so swift and surprising that the Arabs did not have time to sabotage the facility. Next we captured the key Arab town of Ramleh, south of Lod, as well as the pumping station in Ras el-Ein that supplied water to Jerusalem.

A second truce went into effect on July 19, but the Egyptians broke the truce when they began shelling besieged farms in the Negev.

About this time we received 60 Spitfires from Czechoslovakia, of which 24 were flown to the base at Ramat David. We also received some AT-3 Harvard fighter-trainers, which were equipped with a machine gun and bomb racks under the wings. These planes were most welcome, as we had almost depleted our supply of Me-109s due to bad landings and a lack of spare parts. There were other sources of aircraft as well. Although there was a U.S. embargo on all arms sent to the Middle East, we had many "good-will ambassadors" abroad. These included Al Shwimmer and Sy Semakh, Americans who helped us to obtain some large aircraft. Our Air Force now began to look more formidable. Had we had these planes and equipment earlier in 1948, the Arab Legion would never have crossed the Jordan River and East Jerusalem would never have fallen.

In October of 1948, Ben-Gurion ordered an all-out offensive against the Egyptians in the Negev. This time we were better equipped, and we attacked with coordinated artillery and armor. We struck so fast that one of the Egyptian brigades, whose operations officer happened to be Major (and subsequently President of Egypt) Gamal Abdel Nasser, became trapped at a Palestinian village called Faluja. The Israelis gave the Egyptian forces in the so-called "Faluja Pocket" a chance to surrender, but they refused. The Air Force was called in and continually pounded the Egyptian position at the Faluja police fortress. I recall servicing the AT-3's that flew the sorties. The pilots took off, dropped their bombs, and returned to the base. We then reloaded the planes with the pilot in the cockpit and the engine running, and they took off again.

After holding out for four months, the Egyptians finally surrendered the fortress, returning to Egypt in trucks flying white flags. This was after Israel and Egypt signed the Rhodes Armistice Agreement on February 24, 1949, which was to be followed by agreements with Lebanon, Jordan, and Syria. Moshe and I later went to see the fortress. Its walls were full of holes from shrapnel.

In order to complete the expulsion of the Egyptians from the Negev, Israel launched Operation Horev in December of 1948. This operation was aimed at deceiving the enemy to think that an all-out attack was going to commence on the stronger prong of the Egyptian forces in the west. The Egyptians promptly pulled in the second prong for reinforcements. The IDF then surprised the Egyptian flank by using a little-known old Roman road that cut directly across the desert.

The Egyptians put up a stiff resistance. Israeli armor and several seasoned brigades from the north joined in the attack, and captured one fortress after another. The Egyptian Air Force was called in to assist their ground forces, but they met with little success. In the end the Egyptians carried out a hasty retreat, leaving behind hundreds of vehicles. Our forces used the Egyptian trucks to pursue the fleeing army into the Sinai Desert. This created some confusion for our Air Force pilots, who at one point attacked our own units in the belief that they were Egyptians. At the same time, IDF commando units moved in behind the Egyptian lines and cut off their supplies and communications. Israeli forces advanced all the way to El-Arish in the Sinai.

Around the end of December I received orders to report to my commanding officer. The CO told me that the Egyptians had left a Spitfire at El-Arish, and I was asked to inspect the aircraft in order to determine whether it could be flown. However, I was not informed that El-Arish was in the no-man's land that separated our forces from those of the Egyptians.

I was introduced to Dan Tolkovsky, a pilot who was to fly the plane if this was at all possible. We were issued a military truck and assigned seven riflemen for our protection—all of whom were new immigrants who had received only a few hours of military training. Only Dan and I spoke Hebrew. Some of the soldiers spoke Russian, and the others spoke Polish, Yiddish and Bulgarian.

I took my toolbox and we left at dawn, traveling south towards Beersheba and the Sinai. Tolkovsky, who was later to become the head of the Israeli Air Force, did not talk much. Still, I was able to find out that he had been a pilot in the RAF and had flown Spitfires during the war.

The road south was littered with burned-out Egyptian armored vehicles. Some of the vehicles had crude paintings on them—Stars of David that had been stabbed with a dagger dripping blood.

As we continued south I stood on the seat of the truck watching for enemy aircraft from the machine gun turret. In the event of attack from the air we were to abandon the truck and take cover in a ditch. When we arrived in Beer-sheba, a place where Abraham once dug a well to water his flock, we found only a few one-story houses and a dusty street. Today, of course, it is a large and vibrant city.

On the way south we passed a number of burning Egyptian vehicles, some of them with corpses in them. Towards the evening we reached our forces in El-Arish. But before we had a chance to report to the commanding officer, seven Egyptian Spitfires appeared on the horizon. The Spitfires managed to drop a couple of bombs near the headquarters building and then all of the planes came in low with their machine guns blazing. Our escorts were not trained to fire on diving aircraft and did not know how to react. I grabbed one of their rifles, and so did Dan. We lay on our backs behind a sand dune, propped up our legs to rest our rifles on them, and fired away at the diving planes. After each pass, we took shelter on the other side of the sand dune and continued firing. The soldiers who had accompanied us soon learned from our example and opened fire with their weapons. Other soldiers were also shooting at the planes. After several more passes the planes left.

We reported to the commander of the area and he suggested that because the plane was on an exposed runway in no-man's land it would be safest to wait until nightfall to inspect it. After sunset, three jeeps with mounted Browning machine guns escorted us to the aircraft. When I reached the plane I was able to determine quickly that it could not be flown out. The Egyptians had sabotaged it by knocking a hole in the reduction gear, damaging the cockpit window and the starter, and removing the battery. I nevertheless suggested that we take the plane with us. The unit commander, a big guy with two bandoleers of machine gun belts across his chest, gave me a puzzled look. "How are you going to do that?" he asked. I had a couple of soldiers help me lift the plane's tail onto a jeep and secure the tail wheel behind the jeep's tailgate. Then I stationed two men at the wing tips to protect them from brush or sand dunes. I got into the cockpit to oversee the operation. As we left the Egyptians fired some shots in our direction, but they were way off target. Thus we towed the Spitfire behind our lines.

When we got back to the base, we received applause and pats on the back. We radioed Tel Nof to send an aircraft transport truck and some men to help dismantle the wings and remove the 20mm cannons and machine guns. In Tel Nof the plane was repaired and a few days later it joined the ranks of the Spitfire Squadron.

With the IDF in pursuit of the Egyptians in the Sinai, strong diplomatic pressure was brought to bear against the Israeli government. Britain threatened to come to the aid of the Egyptians unless the Israelis withdrew, but fighting continued in spite of this warning. The enemy was being squeezed back when the Egyptian government declared that it was willing to open armistice negotiations. A cease fire went into effect the next day, January 7, 1949. That same day, however, five British fighters came in low over the battlefield on a reconnaissance flight. Our Air Force fighters shot them down, which provoked an angry response from the British government. Fighting continued to occur in sporadic outbursts, but although the Egyptians still held the Gaza Strip the Egyptian campaign was for the most part over.

In 1949, the Arab nations gradually came to the realization that they had been defeated by Israel. The armistice agreement between Israel and Egypt, which was signed in February, was followed by agreements with Lebanon, Jordan, and finally, in July, with Syria. Israel had prevailed in its first war with its Arab neighbors. Unfortunately there were many wars to come, and the ever-present threat of renewed conflict, as well as the reality of Palestinian terrorism, continues to plague the citizens of the Jewish homeland.

By the end of the war, my parents were well settled and seemed quite happy. My father had opened a shoe repair store and was now doing good business. When I came home during weekends we caught up on lost time. I built a radio for my parents and a table lamp made from Plexiglas. They were so proud of it that they showed it off on every occasion. I also encouraged them to learn Hebrew, and they did so quite satisfactorily. I felt proud to see my parents becoming Israelis. Moshe also visited often and the four of us began once again to feel like a close family. But whenever someone brought up the past, Mama cried for the loss of her mother, brother, and other relatives in the Holocaust.

The Air Force and the IDF had made tremendous progress, but more training was needed in order for us technicians to become the best we could be. I was selected along with forty-two other airmen to go to the United States in order to study air frame and engine mechanics at the Spartan School of Aeronautics in Tulsa, Oklahoma. In preparation for our journey we were sent to the army base at Kfar Sirkin for a course in American customs and ethics. We also received some instruction in technical English. We were then issued Israeli passports. Before we left I had to sign a contract with the Air Force for five years. At the time I was planning to make the Air Force my career, so I readily agreed. In December of 1949 I left for the U.S.

Our training at Spartan was excellent. The instruction we received there filled in many gaps in my knowledge of aircraft maintenance and repair. The Tulsa Jewish community was outstandingly supportive and did its best to make us feel at home. We graduated with honors and received A&P (air frame and power plant) licenses after passing the Federal Aviation Administration test. I was asked if I wanted to stay for another three months to take a flight engineering course, but I refused. I felt that if I stayed I would probably have to teach at the Air Force technical school in Haifa, which I did not wish to do.

When I got back to Israel I found that much had changed. The Air Force had acquired several squadrons of P-51 fighters and much new equipment. I was assigned to be in charge of the Air Force engine overhaul facility and was promoted to the rank of Warrant Officer. I had the option to go to officer's training school for six months, but opted not to. As a Warrant Officer with a grade D trade rating my salary was equal to that of a Major. Had I gone to officer's school I would have had to start out as Second Lieutenant. I also had plans to get married.

I met Shirley Cohen at the Tulsa ice skating rink, and we fell in love shortly thereafter. Shirley was a native Tulsan with a happy disposition and lovable character. When I first met her I knew that we would marry. She was graduating from Central High School and getting ready to attend the University of Tulsa. Six months after my return to Israel, Shirley and her mother came to Tel Aviv and we were married at the Dan Hotel on August 27, 1951 in the presence of our families and all of my friends from the Air Force.

Afterword

When I think about my life, so many of my experiences, large as well as small, seem to have faded away. Yet these experiences become real and vivid for me as soon as I read what I have written here. I began to write about the events recorded in this book when they were still fresh in my memory and in the minds of my family and friends—most of whom are now gone.

Today, I cannot imagine myself doing the things I did when I was a boy. But I am not the same person I was sixty years ago. Even my name is different. I changed Goldman to Golan in 1951, and I changed my first name to Bob when I became an American citizen in 1957.

Those who were unable to leave behind a life of peace and comfort did not survive the years of war and exile. I'm glad I made it through those hard times, and I know that I could not have done so without the help of my family. Maybe I, too, helped others along the way. In any case, I learned things from my experiences that I could not have learned otherwise.

My character was forged by the harsh realities of war, including hunger, poverty, and disease. I learned to be selfish and mistrustful, and when necessary to lie and steal. I do not have many regrets, for I was only a boy when we fled from Poland into the Soviet Union. I only hope that I did not hurt anyone, and if I did, I hope they forgave me.

I do not hate as I used to, but I cannot forgive the Germans for what they did. I still grieve for the millions of Jews they murdered, especially the children. Like me, most of those children would have grown up, gotten married, and had children and grandchildren of their own. How many of them or their descendants would have become scientists, physicians, artists, writers, and leaders in a multitude of fields? They had no chance to show the world what they could do, and mankind is immeasurably impoverished by their absence.

As for me, I survived Hitler and Stalin and contributed to the birth of Israel. After two thousand years, a language and a historic homeland were reborn. The events I lived through were unheard of in the annals of history, and I played a part in them.

You can say I survived by my wits, or with the help of others, or by means of plain luck. In fact, it was a combination of all three. In any case, I feel fortunate to have witnessed one of the most important and interesting periods in human history.

Bob Golan
August, 2004

About the Author

After receiving an honorable discharge from the Israeli Air Force in 1954, **Bob Golan** worked for the Israel Aircraft Industries. He subsequently managed several stores and worked as a senior buyer for Otasco in Tulsa Oklahoma. He is married to a native Tulsan, Shirley, and has two sons, Mike and Gary, and two grandchildren. He is now retired and his hobbies include reading, attending lectures, playing golf, and being a handyman. He is a volunteer and occasional speaker at the Tulsa Air and Space Museum.

Jacob Howland is McFarlin Professor of Philosophy at the University of Tulsa. He has published two books, *The Republic: The Odyssey of Philosophy* (New York: Twayne, 1993; reprinted by Paul Dry Books, 2004) and *The Paradox of Political Philosophy: Socrates' Philosophic Trial* (Lanham, MD: Rowman & Littlefield, 1998), and has recently completed a book manuscript entitled *Kierkegaard and Socrates: A Study of Philosophy and Faith*. He is a member of the Tulsa Jewish community and is an active participant in Holocaust education programs in Oklahoma.